The Relationship Dismount

How To Stick The Landing When Exiting A Toxic Relationship

by

RENARD "ZO" WILLIAMS

Published by Dragon-Phoenix Moor Publishing Company

ISBN: 978-0-578-16415-1

First published by Dragon-Phoenix Moor Publishing Company July 2015

Printed in the United States of America
10 9 8 7 6 5 4 3 2 1

Dedication

Thanks to all my failed relationships.
This gift came from you.

In Gratitude

I would like to thank each of you for your seed toward this book. Your financial contribution has made it possible for me to make a difference by sharing this message and shining a light that can be seen and heard. The selfless gift you have given will cause transformation in the lives of many and they will have a self-revelation of their true value. My appreciation runs deeper than you will ever know.

1mwh78
A Obare Cornwell
ahansb05
Ahmad Mussenden
Aint Nice
Aint Nicedeandrewila
ajones110792
ajrussell32
akintunde.bowden
al.spencer
amenrahkay
Andrea Simpson
angie.levelle
anitrasan
apeacock117
apeacock2
artbyodell
BassReeves2015
bigspell1
bineauxeyewear
birukedoc
bloveprohet

bm1800blk
Brandon Walker
brandonrussell79
brianroc11
Britton Harper-DjSkywalker
bryan.joseph
bschell3210
buddhastrike
bwnum13
Byron Vaughn III
Carl Jones
Carleton Coleman
chad.thomas
Channing8806
Charles Williams
charvijanae
chjetplane20
chop44hut
Claude Harton
cljohn2010
Clyde Harris
cmak2k4
confidencemagnet
cordarodavis
corneliusb30
Cory Moore
cpp.hmuhammad
crumbleyjr
ctminimahjr
Cynt Ervin
dan.c.green2
Daniel Lister
danielle1
darielmtaylor
david hampton
David Robinson
davuceo

dclyte07
dd_atk
ddrayton1977
Deacon Aly
*delnorwood b_*
Dennis Beshears
dharris10879
djgetbuck
dlohara1911
Donald Alvarez
dorblack21
E Lavaniel S
Elgin Sincere
elilavalier
Esh Abdulrahmann
Eternal Artist
ethomp163
etmaynevillain
eyeinsee
eyeinsee82
ezimmerman15
fabulusunderground
Fair-Rose Louverture
faygriff3
fleezygraphics
forsudden
fowlermark10
garcapone2002
gcbrhs405
George Reed
glc23bat
granvillebarrett1
greedy4success
grierinc
houchins.sarah
hurvensmonestime
hwharton

hyongosi
idcong12
ihilani78
Ilacy
itsogone
j_christian_hodges
jamalrobinsonlucas
Jamar Wise
James Cain
Jarryl Lawrence
jas_king
jaschancellor
Jason Ware
jatkinson
jchandler3000
jermarsmith90
jleecloak1
Joe MichealsXavier Fairley
John Kushman
john.kuchinski
jollydeqwan
jonahlevien
Joseph Baker
Joshua Torregano
jstink504
jtrigg88
JUNE HUDSON
Kace Moon
Kareem Austin
kareemfolkes1
karlethag
Khalil Sultan
khardyncm
Kojo Cole-Kesse
Kolyn Mincey
kskbowman
kwameellis29

l.terrance
Lance Howard
libraLcloud
lj.lorenzojunior.wright
llkoolday
loneblackwolf86
lottsalexander
louchatman
lovely247
ltm376
mahoganymyers85
Mahzee
Marc Ptah
marcelanderson4
Marcus Williams
Marion Randolph
markduckett0
markesebrown08
Marlon Green
marshea_lowe
maximelavieestbelle
mfewser
mianeema
Michael Blaktroy667788
Middx Pious
Miron Clay-Gilmore
missgilly77
monice1872
Montele Wesley
Morris
mustafa.a.alamin
myoussef1991
neterankhhotep-el
ng160001a
noregretmedia
nthnycrutcher502
nuneeq

onterrybell
orlando.humble
Parris Brantley
pasdilworth8
pengepete
perfectcirclezane
pettybone123
preciousgills
Providence Grupee
Que Hampton
randycurtis7
Rasheed Sulaiman
Raymond Peyton
raynacrawford
realalvin1978
Reggie Simon
Renaissance Ric
Richard Norman
rickdoss122008
Ricky Massey
ritagranberry
rjbradle
Robert Overstreet
ronald.walton
rondrickcapehart
Ronin Martin
Rupert French
screen23_2003
Sedri Webst
semeon.charles
shadowalker34
shante6265
shanton1981
shaysw24
Sherman Lowery
Sherron Robinson
simsjohn1

smallscorey3184
ssmedical1
stephanie pegues
stevewhitestl
strongarm80
studiosevendesign
sullivan young jr
Tasha M
tburgh2053
Tenise Dry
thatboygoodsp
Thomas Shields
Tim Smith II
tmaj12k
tmhonesty
transium biggquis
Travis Minter
Tripolle James
tyhon83 J
unbreakablehobby
unitedfreedom
Veronica Conway
Wally Pocs
warrior69315
Wayne Locke
*wdavis_jr_*
wegj62001
wes.holloway614
westcity04
william.church711
wizziewaz1
wpbarnette
xavieruncle34
Yovonda McDaniel
yungd2006
Zondo Sakala

THE RELATIONSHIP DISMOUNT

Foreword

I first met Zo Williams when I appeared as a guest on his *Voice of Reason* radio show on Jamie Foxx's Foxxhole Radio Network. His smartness, passion, and "heart" had me at "hello"! I have felt pleased, honored, and privileged at his having me follow him as a co-host on the #Zo What? Radio Show; first on the Roscoe Media Center radio and more recently on TradioV.

I can't remember knowing a better, more widely read individual with a capacity to "go deeper" on nearly any topic--even though that is a prompt to his guests and co-hosts.

But I digress...which if I did on the show, Zo would have respectfully, but in no uncertain terms, gotten me back on track! And the track I am on here is to urge you to read his amazing book, *The Relationship Dismount: How to Stick the Landing When Exiting a Toxic Relationship.*

As a fellow relationship expert two catchy phrases have played over and over again through my mind regarding relationships that I have for years wished someone would write a book about.

The first notion is that "relationships are presumed dead." By that I mean that the moment you start to presume things about another person you begin to assume and then expect that other person to act in a certain way. Most of the time, what leads you to presuming is that you are focused on an idea of who the other person should be instead of who they really are. Zo often says on the show, and now in this book, *"Don't date your ideas."*

In the book, Zo does an amazing job of teaching you how to stop presuming about others by truly getting to know what Michael Jackson kept referring to as "The Man in the Mirror." By learning to know who you are, what drives you, and what blinds you, you develop the possibility to love another person for *who* they are instead of only loving them for *how* they make you feel. The latter approach can only end in failure.

The other phrase that has stuck with me with regard to relationships is "press pause to play." By that I mean you need to find ways to "curb your enthusiasm" before it becomes a "runaway train" that threatens to steamroll anyone in your path and destroy your chance for a lasting relationship.

In addition to the wise and sage guidance in this book, you will find exercises that, if you take the time to do, will slow you down enough to pause and make better choices in your relationships that are reasonable, make sense, and realistic and have a chance of actually working out.

Read this book over and over and I promise you that you will discover your own "Voice of Reason" and with that, have the chance for a relationship where you and the person who is fortunate to be your partner can love happily ever after. And it won't be a fairy tale.

Dr. Mark Goulston, M.D.
Author of *Just Listen: Discover the Secret to Getting Through to Absolutely Anyone* and Co-host of *The #Zo What? Morning Show*

Table of Contents

Chapter 1

What Can Your Relationships Show You About You?...1

Chapter 2

Relationship As a Vehicle: Being Transformed In and Through Relationships 15

Chapter 3

In the Cocoon | Information Space of Mental Openness and Awareness 31

Chapter 4

Self-Reflection and Self-Examination 43

Chapter 5

Accountability | Letting Go of Blame and Powerlessness... 59

Chapter 6

Forgiveness | Letting Go of Shame and Guilt 75

Chapter 7

Landing Well | Shedding Regret 89

Chapter 8

Chapter 9

Chapter 10

Chapter 11

Rebooting the Relationship from a Transformed Perspective 147

Chapter 12

Tying It All Together.............................. 165

THE RELATIONSHIP DISMOUNT

Thank Yous
And Acknowledgments

To my mother Rosetta Evonne Walker/Williams, James and Mary Bynum, Shatoune N. Shepard, Maurice Raynard Williams, James Rodney Williams, Cassandra Williams, Kool Mo Dee, James Gus Lewis, Nuwr'Iyl Elijah Williams, Prema Emani Williams, Na'im Nasir Muhammad, Anthony Williams, Daa'Iyah Muhammad, Valerie Williams, Stephney Riley, Karyn Folan, Lynn Pace, Carolyn Reynolds, Queen Jahneen Etter, and Joy Alantis Marshall. If your name does not appear on this shortlist it doesn't mean that your contribution to my life was insignificant; on the contrary, it simply means there's not enough space to write about the enormity of the impact your presence had on my life.

THE RELATIONSHIP DISMOUNT

Chapter 1

What Can Your Relationships Show You About You?

> *Tanaya squinted at the crinkled subway map.*
>
> *"What train should I take?" she wondered aloud.*
>
> *"It depends," a woman near her answered, "on where you're coming from and where you're going."*

Getting On and Off the Love Train

Relationships can be likened to all forms of transportation, even the train that Tanaya is waiting for. Our relationships can take us many places. Sometimes we delight in the journey and hope the trip never ends. Other times, we're impatient for the expected destination. When the trip is miserable, we may want to get off the train as soon as possible, even if we're not at our intended stop. Sadly, we may also feel, at times, like we've been thrown off the train.

How can we land without stumbling? How can we make good relationships even better? How can we learn to take stock of the lessons learned from our past relationships and move forward, healed and whole, into future relationships?

2

This book was birthed from the death of a romantic relationship. In the midst of the pain of that break up, I realized that I had some choices. I could stuff it all down and pretend that I didn't have any bad feelings. I could wallow in the bad feelings, and lock myself in a prison of anger and misery. Or I could choose to act, instead of just being acted upon by those thoughts of despair. I could be a victor who overcomes, instead of a victim who undergoes the treatment others, and myself, dish out.

Bringing forth good things out of the mess of a broken relationship requires use of my most potent organ of manhood – the squiggly gray one between my ears. As King Solomon said in the proverb, *"As a man thinks, so he is." (See Proverbs 23:7).*

Ladies, it's true for you, too. Our thinking is key to healing (or healing from) bad relationships and nurturing good ones. The eyes, the heart, and parts farther south, might lead us into many a romantic encounter, but it is using our minds that will change us for the better and make us better able to choose relationships wisely, which would enable us to become our best selves in the relationships we choose.

This aforementioned process/relationship routine takes a good deal of mental energy. It takes thinking and reflecting deeply about the meaning of relationships, the hard aspects of relationships, the difficult circumstances/choices that we are not used to facing or considering. Most people don't think about every little aspect of their lives all the time. People often act out of habit/routine, or out of emotional reaction, without giving much (if any) objective thought to what they do or why they are doing it. In a relationship routine that is going well, we might not want to mess up all the good feelings by thinking about it too much. In a relationship routine that has turned sour, we may prefer to think about more pleasant things or ending the relationship routine. On the other hand, we may get caught in cycle of negative thought that, in my opinion, sets up the relationship for a messy dismount. That kind of mindset is a set-up for missing one of the most important opportunities in life.

Intimate relationships equate to transformation, which is a type of transportation on the train of love with the last stop being self-awareness.

The Sporting Life

Think about how great athletes approach their craft. They don't just "wing" it. They, too, have a routine for greatness; that routine may include practice before they play, and after the game is played, watching video from the last game to critique every subtlety and nuance of their performance. Studying game film, the athlete and team emerge with a clearer perspective on what they are trying to accomplish and how to get there.

For instance, take the sport of gymnastics. It is a marriage of artistic passion and athletic technique. During the performance, the gymnast soars through the routine before a spellbound audience. But every exhilarating flight must have a landing, and the gymnast's landing is paramount to the success of the overall routine. The landing is the last picture in the audience's mind. The dismount should be solidly planted, a "stuck landing," in gymnastics talk. Stumbling or even moving the feet during the landing will cost the competitive gymnast crucial points.

Landing well is just as important when a relationship routine hits a plateau. Are you gearing up for the next phase? Or is it time for closure? Wisely executed relationship dismounts build strong foundations for future relationships. Ragged dismounts make for shaky foundations and make it more likely that unexamined baggage and relationship debris will undermine new relationships in the future.

With the mindset of an athlete, we can learn to harvest good things from relationships, even from hard or painful ones. We can learn to identify attitudes and behaviors that are holding us back from being our best and happiest selves. We can figure out what is worth keeping, what we need to stop doing, or to start doing differently.

The harvest begins by looking at where we have come from.

Beginnings: From One Basket to Another

I'll start with the subject I know best – my own beginnings. Later on, you can take a deeper look at your own beginnings. Understanding where we come from can help us discover why we look at some things the way we do and why we tend to respond in certain ways to people and situations.

Many of the circumstances and relationships I experienced in my early years were less than ideal. I was born in Chattanooga, Tennessee in the early 1970s, the sixth and last child of my 27- year-old mother. Though my mother only married the first of the three men who fathered her six children, we were each given the last name of Williams, the name of the biological father of my three oldest siblings, notwithstanding Mr. Williams' absence during most of their lives. I believe that, by giving all her children the same last name, my mother tried to create a sense of cohesion in an otherwise confusing scenario.

This fragile family structure disintegrated when my mother experienced a mental breakdown three months after my birth. The four youngest children went to live with family members or in foster care, situations that were far from ideal, but were still better than our destitute life in the Alton Park Projects. My two oldest brothers were considered too old to enter the foster care system, so they had to endure group home living conditions that smacked of punishment and incarceration.

My older brother, who is only 10 months older than me, was placed into the foster home of James and Mary Bynum, a suburban

Chattanooga couple who had previously raised many other foster children. Initially unaware that their new foster child had a younger sibling, the Bynums inquired about the existence of the "baby brother" their new foster child kept talking about. I had not yet been placed in a foster home, and when the Bynums found me, vulnerable and lying listlessly in a basket, they determined that I would not remain alone and made sure my brother and I were reunited in their caring home.

Life in the Bynum household was incredibly ideal. My brother and I lived in a genuinely supportive, well-balanced and generous environment. We attended worship services each week, and the Bynums gave us nice, new clothing and taught us good grooming. Birthday and Christmas presents were always in abundance. The first five years of my life were picture perfect, and I never imagined that these loving parents were not my biological parents. Further, I couldn't even begin to comprehend that the "nice lady" that we would visit occasionally, was actually our biological mother.

My mother was released from the mental facility just a few short months after my siblings and I were placed in various dwellings, and Mrs. Bynum would regularly see my mother around town. During one of these chance encounters, Mrs. Bynum sensed in my mother such emptiness and despair over the loss of custody of her youngest children that Mrs. Bynum felt compelled to find a way to reunite us with our mother. Soon after that conversation, my brother and I were sent back to live permanently with our biological mother, who had been residing in the Alton Park Projects for over a decade.

To describe as a "struggle" the transition from suburban life to project living would be an understatement. At the age of five, I was torn from the safe cocoon of the Bynum's' well-manicured, immaculate home and thrust into the fear, uncertainty and confusion of life in the projects with the strangers who made up my "real" family. While the Bynums had taught my brother and me to be polite, respectful and cordial, my fifteen-year-old brother, an intimidating figure, saw fit to re-socialize, and indoctrinate us into ways of thinking and acting that were more conducive to survival in the projects.

In retrospect, I think he was trying to protect us. When my older brother looked at my brother and me, he saw two vulnerable, polished suburban young boys with physical characteristics that he knew would render us targets if he didn't toughen us up immediately. I learned to love to fight, to travel by rooftops and sewers when the streets were too dangerous, and generally to be streetwise, evasive and untrusting. I learned to carry my older sister piggyback across the kitchen floor at night, to keep her away from the roaches and rats that congregated there in frightening numbers.

My brother tried to mentor me and serve as sort of a father figure, but he struggled with his own anger and resentment due to his father's absence and the harsh treatment he experienced in the group home. Since he had not yet overcome his own struggles, he could not help passing on the influence of those struggles to his interactions with me.

My mother eventually grew weary of our grim circumstances. When I was around eight years old, my mother decided to move the family to Altadena, California, where my eldest brother lived in a two-bedroom apartment. My mother packed up the remaining family with all the food and possessions we could carry, and we boarded a Trailways bus for the cross-country trip to Southern California.

Adapting to California living was hard. The aggressive fighting skills that served me well in the Alton Park Projects were ill suited to the extremely laid back nature of Southern California. I became very angry, not knowing what was "right," and facing yet another confusing experience of adaptation and re-socialization. I was kicked out of elementary school for fighting just a few months after enrolling.

After several years of living in Altadena and attending different schools, my family finally settled in Pasadena. It was there that I was able to find my first love: basketball. Basketball provided me an outlet to release many of my frustrations, and the basketball court became my haven of solace and inner peace.

How Do We Learn about Ourselves?

We are all born in the middle of circumstances. Your life curriculum (experience) may be happy, hard, chaotic or painful. Either way, our experiences affect how we think about ourselves and how we think about the world around us. Those experiences create a lens, like a pair of ever-changing glasses that we look through. We tend to interpret our next experiences based on our interpretation of our previous experiences.

What do we think we see?

Why do we think we see it?

One question to ask is, *"It is possible that the lenses I have built throughout my life are actually distorting my perception?"* If we take time to examine the glasses, clean them off, and try to fix places where they are warped, we will see better and more accurately. Greater insight can bring clearer focus, which can bring even greater insight, which can bring even clearer focus, and so on.

Another way we learn about ourselves is by looking at how other people respond to us. In a way, our relationships with other people are like mirrors in which we see a reflection of ourselves. In fact, we might even think of relationships as classrooms – highly reflective classrooms – in which we learn about ourselves, and our partners learn about themselves.

We have to be wise and careful about what we do with this reflected information from others. Just as our own perspectives and perceptions can be distorted, so can the perceptions and perspectives of other people. People don't respond to us so much as they respond to their perceptions, expectations and interpretations of who we are, what we do, and why we do it. We have to test the accuracy and fidelity of the information we get reflected in the responses and reactions of others. But there is a wealth of information there, if we will take the time to sift and sort through it.

Sifting Through My Story

Now that you know the basics about the story of the early years of my life, you may have already identified some significant events and patterns.

My healthiest relationship was with the Bynums (foster parents) during my first five years. That relationship taught me what it was like to be valued and how to interact with people in a safe environment. It was a relationship full of good things. The only challenging aspect about that relationship was its abrupt end, and the bewildering discovery that the Bynums were not my real parents. Those elements left me questioning the stability and certainty of what I thought I knew.

My relationship with my biological father was virtually non-existent. I last spoke with him when I was thirteen. His absence left me feeling rejected, abandoned and angry. It also left a void where a male role model should be. My second oldest brother tried to fill that void, and the good thing about my relationship with him was that he cared enough about me to try to protect me and teach me the best he knew how. The potentially damaging part was that his instruction was long on toughening and short on nurturing, and it was not adaptable to markedly different environments. What equipped me somewhat well for life in the projects backfired in Southern California, and once again, I was angry and confused when I did what I was taught to do, but it didn't work and wasn't "right," when and where I tried to apply it. Expulsion from school was yet another kind of rejection that grew from the mix of mutually exclusive behaviors I had assimilated.

My relationship with my mother was complex. She tried to make a better life for us in California. By wanting us back, she made it clear she was not rejecting us. Yet she was so weakened by her own brokenness and her own unresolved relationships that she was unable to provide a lighthouse in the storm. I wonder how different my own youth might have been if she and my father (and the other two men who fathered my siblings) had been able to accomplish a clean, strong "landing" from their relationship routines, and move forward in wholeness and peace.

Taking this hard look into my past brings insight. I can see that I carry into new relationships the tendency toward anger, especially when I feel rejected or questioned about the integrity of my actions. I am slower to trust and believe in the permanence of relationships, and I keep re-evaluating the validity of what I think I know. The anger can turn good relationships into train wrecks. The caution that comes with delayed trust has good and bad side effects. Wisdom, prudence, and open-mindedness are good qualities that contribute to stable relationships and to growth as a person, but deficiencies in trust and shifting foundations of perception can undermine the durability of a relationship and the partners' confidence in the relationship and in each other.

For me, it's important to know where I've been, but I am not bound or limited by the knowledge of my past. Mining insights from my past often lead me to questions that can bring about fulfilling changes in my understanding of myself.

Do I want to keep getting angry? What thoughts can I choose to think when I feel the venom of anger welling up in me? What are the things that I think I know about the origin of my anger? What can I set down as bedrock for the way I see the world? What perceptions are trustworthy? What perceptions need changing? How can I reinterpret my past and chart a course for the future, based on more reliable perceptions and belief systems? Most of all, what kind of man do I want to be? How can I be that man in my personal and professional life? How do I want to interact with my romantic partner and with my children?

EXERCISE 1: PUTTING THESE IDEAS INTO PRACTICE

Now it's your turn.

What are the golden nuggets from your past that you want to keep? What are the things that need facing and changing? These questions may help you start your own journey.

Think of three people whose relationships with you, past or present, are having the biggest impact on your life right now.

     1. _____

     2. _____

     3. _____

For each of the three key relationships you picked, answer the following questions:

What is/was fulfilling, uplifting, and self-educating about that relationship?

_____

_____

What is/was challenging, traumatic, and/or painful about that relationship?

_____

_____

What would you change about that relationship, if you could?

_____

What would you do differently in that relationship (or in a similar relationship) in the future?

_____

_____

Describe the way you see yourself now.

I am: _____

Describe the way you want to be.

I want to be: _____

What do you think it will take to get from the way you see yourself now to the way you want to be?

_____

_____

To get to where I want to be:

I will keep doing _____

I will stop doing _____

I will start doing _____

WHAT CAN YOUR RELATIONSHIPS SHOW YOU ABOUT YOU?

Chapter 2

Relationship As a Vehicle: Being Transformed In and Through Relationships

> *The ultimate goal in a relationship is to learn about yourself and serve your partner.*

People sometimes misunderstand the purpose of relationships. Out of that misunderstanding, they may break up prematurely when the relationship becomes difficult, without a solid reason for why they should break up and without really understanding what the relationship is or isn't providing them.

As we will discover in this chapter, our relationships function as a highly reflective classroom. Most relationships start based on attraction, or physical and emotional connectivity. But at a deeper level, relationships actually provide curriculum for you. The curriculum is based on who you are, and what you need to learn comes from what the person you're dating reflects back to you, like a mirror. When I say relationship is a classroom, I mean that the purpose of a relationship (for both people in the relationship) is to learn about themselves through some of the difficulties that manifest themselves in the process of being in a relationship. You have probably heard the old saying, *"You never really know a person until you live with them."* Even more, I think it's true that you never really know yourself until you face the reflections of yourself that come back from a relationship with another person. These reflections might be things that you never liked about yourself or they might be things you never even knew were there until the relationship revealed them.

When my oldest son was a 15-year-old varsity basketball player in 10th grade, I told him, *"Listen, relationship is a class that you will never graduate from, so take your time before you enroll into this class. It's the toughest class you're ever going to take."*

I want him to understand that relationships are not all about instant gratification. They are not all about status — like my girl being the prettiest girl or my husband being the most powerful or the wealthiest. Relationships are a classroom where the curriculum is self-oriented, so that each person in the relationship can get self-knowledge through the vehicle of relationship. One thing that makes relationships so tough is that they put you face-to-face with yourself, in a highly reflective classroom of not-so-flattering mirrors. Often, people bail out of relationships when they get tough, not understanding that it is the tough times, or that challenging, conflicted nature of relationship that contributes the most to their growth as people. Sometimes we take unchallenged beliefs or outdated perspectives into a relationship because we've never been in a relationship with somebody who could provide an adequate mirror to let us see ourselves clearly enough to recognize that our beliefs or perspectives might need some considering or re-considering. Just because something is uncomfortable or doesn't feel good doesn't mean it isn't good for you. In our fast food society, we tend to go for things that are easy/safe. We tend to go for things that are not challenging and things that feel good. But what we fail to realize is that just because it feels good to you doesn't mean it is good for you. And just because it feels bad to you doesn't necessarily mean it isn't good for you. We don't always like what we see in the mirror. But when we learn to stop running away from the image of ourselves that we don't like to see, and look at it for what it really is, we can finally recognize what we want to change, and what we want to keep. When that recognition turns into action, we make progress toward growth.

The Impossibility of Not Being in Relationship

Philosopher and spiritual teacher Jiddu Krishnamurti started me thinking about how fundamental relationships are and what we discover and learn from them[1]. He said, *"Life is relationship, which is expressed through contact with things, with people, and with ideas. In understanding relationship, we shall have the capacity to meet life fully, adequately…Relationship, surely, is the mirror in which you discover yourself. Without relationship you are not; to be is to be related; to be related is existence[i]."*

As I have thought about these ideas, I have come to realize that relationships are a kind of classroom – a highly reflective classroom – that can reveal insight, understanding, and can produce transformation. That classroom is all around us; everywhere we go, because there are always other people around us, with whom we stand in relationship.

Ubuntu – I Am Because We Are

Most of this book discusses romantic relationships, or at least, our closest and most intimate relationships, such as those with family and close friends. The true web of relationship is wider than that, though. We may influence and inform those we may never meet face-to-face, and they, too, may influence and inform us. There

---

[1] *I am deeply indebted to insights I have gained from the teachings of Krishnamurti. But since his philosophy emphasized the individual's own uncharted journey to truth, the step-by-step process that we are unfolding in this book is a clear departure from an essential part of the views he expressed.*

can also be a tendency to view a relationship as a closed system, like a very small exclusive club with only two members. Even with the intensity of being involved with another person, it is important to remember that a person does not stop being *in relationship* with others just because he or she is *in an intimate relationship* with a special someone.

Writing in the early 1600s, John Donne described this wider web of relationships this way: *"No man is an island, entire of itself; every man is a piece of the continent... any man's death diminishes me, because I am involved in mankind[ii]..."* Relationship is inescapable, not just with our family, friends and loved ones, but with all of our fellow human beings and all that is part of our world.

In the Southern African region, there's a concept of *Ubuntu*, which is sometimes translated as *"I am because we are,"* one's identity as a person is essentially tied to others in community. According to Michael Onyebuchi Eze, *"a person's humanity is dependent on the appreciation, preservation, and affirmation of another person's humanity. To deny another's humanity is to depreciate my own humanity[iii]."*

While there are many dimensions, and various translations (sometimes contradicting ones) of the term Ubuntu, which extend into political and cultural philosophies far beyond the scope of this book, the key point for me is that individuals engage with other individuals in the context of community, in ways that contribute to the ongoing development of both the individuals involved and the community as well.

Relationship as Related-ness

In 1802, astronomer William Herschel wrote about a certain pair of stars that, *"remain united by the bond of their own mutual gravitation towards each other[iv].*" Today, we call these "binary stars." They revolve around each other, sort of like two people do when they first fall in love.

Most people are so selfish they think every relationship is about them. A relationship is not just about you. It's about your partner, too. A relationship is a dyadic experience where you each give something to the other and each get something from the other.

Some relationships stay like binary stars. The people involved tend to stay in each other's orbit and they have an ever-deepening sense that they are supposed to be together, like cornerstones in each other's lives. Cornerstones might be lifelong friends (authentic BFFs) or what we think of as "soul-mates" that progress from being passionate young lovers to old people holding hands in their rocking chairs. The gravitational pull between them doesn't diminish as time passes or as circumstances change. My interpretation of a cornerstone relationship is one where the people involved have a seemingly inexhaustible ability to keep giving, receiving and accepting from each other without judgment of the highly reflective curriculum that comes from being in relationship.

Sometimes with certain friendships or romantic relationships the gravitational pull of attraction fades over time. Perhaps you have a specific thing to give to and receive from each other in that moment in time, and once that giving and receiving is done, you can graciously move on. You are more like stepping-stones in each other's lives, without the permanence and continuity of cornerstones[2].

As long as people in stepping-stone relationships are committed to serving each other instead of misusing each other, there is no

---

[2] *I am indebted to Kool Mo Dee for his contributions as co-creator of the terminology and concept of cornerstone relationships and stepping stone relationships.*

inherent harm in stepping-stone relationships. The chief problem arises when the partners have different, and inflexible, expectations about the relationship. Let's face it; no one really wants to be identified as a "BFFN" (Best Friend For Now), or "SMFN" (Soul Mate For Now) or someone's "Mr. or Mrs. Right Now." Sometimes one person wants a cornerstone relationship when the other person may only be looking for the stepping-stone version of relationship. Other times the intensity of a stepping-stone relationship (during its "season") makes the people involved mistake the relationship for a cornerstone relationship. Hurt and disappointment come when the intensity and attraction (relationship gravity) diminishes and the people involved begin to move out of each other's orbit.

Cornerstone relationships are the romantic ideal, the stuff that movies and greeting cards are made of. But stepping-stone relationships, rightly perceived, are not second-class relationships. Stepping-stone relationships can be vitally important. What you give and receive in a stepping-stone relationship prepares both of you for the next situation in each of your lives.

I personally believe that, in a way, every relationship has stepping-stone qualities, because you can learn something from everyone you've ever been with. The difference between a stepping-stone and a cornerstone relationship, in my opinion, is that maybe the stepping-stone relationship has a specific lesson to teach you; in a cornerstone relationship, you're always learning something from that person throughout the relationship.

If you want a relationship to help you mount up in Truth, keep in mind that every relationship you enter into is a highly reflective classroom that allows you to grow and expand as a being—whether it lasts forever or six months. Cultivate the personal confidence to understand that your partner does not make you who you are. Your partner helps elucidate who you are and bring the true picture into clearer focus. Once you have a clearer picture of who you are, you can choose to walk in that Truth.

The ultimate goal in a relationship is to learn about yourself and serve your partner. Just as you learn from what your partner reflects back to you, you serve your partner with your reflections.

What and How We Learn from Relationships

What does it mean for relationships to reveal information? Here's an example that might help. Many computers come with games already pre-loaded onto them, and one of these games is called Minesweeper. If you have ever played Minesweeper, you know that the goal of the game is to click on all the empty spaces as quickly as possible, without clicking on a "mine" or a bomb. If you click on a mine, it explodes, and you lose the game.

There are probably a lot of people who play Minesweeper like a guessing game. They click on a square and hope they don't get blown up. If they do get blown up, they just hit reset and start a new game…over and over again.

But Minesweeper is not really a guessing game. Clicking on a square gives the player a lot of information, if the player has the eyes to see it. That's because clicking on a square reveals a number. The number tells the player how many mine-squares the square is touching. In other words, the number is based on the relationship between the square, the player clicked, and the identity (whether it is an empty square or whether it is a mine) of the other squares the clicked square touches.

Once the player has enough of that kind of information, the player can begin to draw conclusions. Good reasoning helps the player act with confidence that the next square clicked will not be a mine, but an empty space that provides even more helpful information. Mistakes in reasoning, or drawing too certain a conclusion from too little information can lead the player to click boldly on a square that actually contains a mine. BOOM! End of game!

The key is what we do with the information we draw from the context of all our relationships. The goal is to let that understanding inform us and enlighten us, but not limit us.

Mirror, Mirror

Michael Jackson sang an incredibly thought-provoking, and critically acclaimed, song for his 1987 Bad album, written by Siedah Garrett and Glen Ballard, called "Man in the Mirror[v]." One of the most moving lyrics was *"I'm starting with the man in the mirror."* What we are starting to see is that the multidimensional and multifaceted mirrors of self-knowledge are all around us. Our relationships with people, things, and ideas are all mirrors, creating a highly reflective classroom that completely envelops us in all aspects of our lives.

I've experienced stepping-stone and cornerstone relationships in different ways. I can remember when I was 25 dealing with a young lady who very well could have been a cornerstone in my life, but I wasn't mature enough to recognize or handle that. At my maturity level I could only handle a stepping-stone—someone who could possibly teach me something, and then I would move on from that situation. But in hindsight, I can see that she had all of the qualities of a cornerstone, and more importantly, she was invested in trying to be a cornerstone for me. That was when I was 25.

When I turned 29, I was dealing with another young lady. She was six years younger than I was. I knew she was a stepping-stone but I wasn't truthful with myself or with her, and it created more problems as the relationship progressed. What I recognized was that the situation felt good. It felt like, *"Oh, this could be long term."* And when I talk about feeling, I just mean sexually. In my spirit I knew this wasn't the situation for me long term. I knew it, but like I said, I wasn't honest. By being dishonest in this situation, by living in an inauthentic manner, I created more conflict that I'm continuing to experience to this day, from that particular person, and rightfully so.

I think Bob Marley said it the best when he said, *"The biggest coward is a man who awakens a woman's love with no intention of loving her*[vi].*"* To apply that idea to my situation, the worst thing you can do is wake a woman up in terms of her loving you and then not be ready to love her back. That's the worst thing you can do, and I did that when I was 29. I dealt with this lady in an intimate relationship from age 29 to 34, and the fallout from my actions and choices are still causing problems today in terms of how she and I speak and interface with one another.

Cornerstone relationships are very tricky. There's a woman that I've been dealing with for the last 17 years, and although the intimate portion of the relationship has been over for seven or eight years now, you could call her a cornerstone because through hell or high water, through thick and thin, she's always been down for me by having my best interest at heart. She has always been a staunch supporter of my endeavors and my well-being, even when I was intimately involved, while still intimately involved with her, for over six years with someone else that I thought was "the one." Through all of it, the one woman who was a true cornerstone in my life with her presence and support, I had ignorantly and mistakenly labeled a stepping-stone.

So is it possible to miss out on something great by not recognizing a real cornerstone relationship? And is it possible to create a painful mess by misleading yourself and the other person to believe that what is really just a stepping-stone relationship is a cornerstone relationship?

Some people reveal themselves to be cornerstones, because like soul mates or twin flames, the connection endures spiritually and energetically beyond the physical circumstances of the relationship. This type of relationship is exceedingly rare.

Too often, we get blinded by building up a societal image of the *"good relationship."* By societal image, I mean a kind of formula that society tells us is a recipe for a successful relationship, but it does not really work in every case. You know how the formula goes.

I guess we must be cornerstones, because:

> We both went to college.

> We both have good jobs.

> We both go to church.

> We both share the same religion.

> We're both attracted to each other.

Unfortunately, it just doesn't work that way. Two people can meet all of society's expectations and benchmarks and still not have that energetic and spiritual union that makes a cornerstone relationship endure. A cornerstone is going to outlive and weather all of the things that hurt us the most in intimate relationships. A cornerstone is going to find the reason for why we love each other when the weather is at its worst. That's a cornerstone. A cornerstone is going to allow unconditional love to heal all hurts, all misunderstandings and all problems. Trust me. You are going to find that experience one day in your life, and you're going to understand that every other experience as a stepping-stone was designed to get you to that understanding, to get you to that experience. That's what a cornerstone is to me.

To be honest with everyone here and now, I've had glimpses of the cornerstone, but I have yet to have the cornerstone in my life. They've come at different times—sometimes I was ready and they weren't, sometimes I wasn't ready and they were. When I was ready, for whatever reason, it didn't work out. So just because it's considered a cornerstone doesn't necessarily mean that it's yours forever or that they'll be there forever. One thing I do know is the love will endure regardless of where they are—in or out of your life.

To bring the point home, I believe that every relationship, as I said earlier, is to be perceived as a self-knowledge classroom. Everybody is a stepping-stone in terms of what you need to learn about yourself at that moment when you attract that particular relationship. Whatever relationship reflection you identify as the trigger, or as the problem, becomes the subject or the curriculum you need to work on inwardly. For me personally, my subject or curriculum would be developing patience and not becoming disappointed when people do not live up to their stated intentions.

I'm the kind of person who takes people at their word. If you say, *"I love you,"* I take you at your word. If you say, *"I care about you,"* I take you at your word. And then when you do something to me that is opposite of what you say, I tend to get pulled into disappointment. So I need to understand that people are not necessarily their word but their intention. Words are a representation of what someone would like to do, but it's not necessarily what they will do. Even with the best of intentions, a person's actions will not necessarily be in alignment with what they say. Recognizing statements as intentions, that may not be actualized, is a lesson that I need to learn.

EXERCISE 2: PUTTING THESE IDEAS INTO PRACTICE

Remember when we talked about the Minesweeper computer game? We saw that it takes a lot of focus and concentration to pull out helpful information from Minesweeper and process that information to make good decisions about the next move to make in the game. In the same way, it takes focus and concentration to make sense out of what we see in all the mirrors around us.

If you have ever been in a funhouse hall of mirrors, you know how confusing it can be to try to get where you are going. It's a good idea to stop while you try to make sense of the information you are getting from all the reflections coming from all of the mirrors.

The "cocoon" is what I call the place where we put everything else on "pause," while we try to sort through all the reflections and what they mean. In the next chapter, we'll talk more about the cocoon and what happens there.

You can go deeper at the end of the next chapter, after we talk about the cocoon. For now, just take a minute to think about how the ideas in this chapter relate to your life and experiences.

Think back to those three people who you identified at the end of the last chapter as having the biggest impact on your life right now. For each person, would you consider that relationship to be a cornerstone relationship or a stepping-stone relationship in your life?

Name: _____

            Cornerstone   Stepping-stone

Name: _____

            Cornerstone   Stepping-stone

Name: _____

Cornerstone   Stepping-stone

For each cornerstone relationship you identified, answer the following questions:

What have I received in the past in this relationship?

_____

_____

What have I given in the past in this relationship?

_____

_____

What am I receiving now in this relationship?

_____

_____

What am I giving now in this relationship?

_____

_____

Why do I consider this relationship to be a cornerstone relationship in my life?

_____

_____

For each stepping-stone relationship you identified, answer the following questions:

What have I learned about myself this relationship?

_____

_____

Why do I consider this relationship to be a stepping-stone relationship in my life?

_____

_____

If your next interaction (in a current relationship or in your next relationship) were a final exam based upon the curriculum in each of the three relationships you discussed, what subject (the area in which you think you learned lessons to help you grow) do you think would be on the exam?

Relationship 1: _____ Final Exam Subject: _____
Relationship 2: _____ Final Exam Subject: _____
Relationship 3: _____ Final Exam Subject: _____

What does the web of relationships in my life show me about me?

_____

_____

What can I discover and conclude from the reflections, reactions, and responses around me?

_____

_____

RELATIONSHIP AS A VEHICLE

Chapter 3

In the Cocoon | Information Space of Mental Openness and Awareness

> *Don't sit back and think that your progress is contingent on someone else's progress, because it isn't.*

A Cocoon

When you hear "cocoon" what do you envision in your mind's eye? Do you see some warm, cozy place where you can curl up and rest? Or do you think, "There's a developing grub or bug in there!" or "If I put it on a hook, can I use it as bait?" What's going on in that cocoon? What will happen when the being inside emerges? What will it be?

When I talk about the cocoon, I mean a place of mental openness and awareness. It is a safe place, where we can have eyes wide open, without fear. It is a place for awareness, where we can be open to seeing truth, even when it is uncomfortable to see and acknowledge. We go to the cocoon for many reasons. We may enter the cocoon to heal from broken relationships. We may enter the cocoon to consider taking our current relationship to the next level.

It may involve a physical space that is free from distraction and that feels safe and comfortable. Mostly, though, the cocoon is a mental, emotional, and spiritual place. It is the place where we do the hard work of change... metamorphosis... transformation. It is the hidden place where worms that once crawled in the dust advance into soaring butterflies.

Caterpillars and Inchworms are on the Way to Becoming Something Else

Many of you may recall a story by Eric Carle called *The Very Hungry Caterpillar*[vii]. Maybe you heard this story as a child, or more recently, you might have read it to a child. It tells the story of a caterpillar with a serious case of the munchies. This caterpillar eats holes through all kinds of healthy food and some not-so-healthy food. After the caterpillar finishes this huge amount of food, it spins a cocoon around itself. Inside the cocoon, away by itself in the dark, the caterpillar begins to process all that it has consumed. But it does more than just digest; it starts to change. When it finally emerges from the cocoon, the caterpillar has transformed into a butterfly.

Like that caterpillar, we have accumulated a lot of stuff during our lives and relationships. Some of it is good, healthy stuff that is suitable for keeping. Some of it is making us sick or is otherwise hindering or stunting our growth and just needs to be jettisoned from one end or the other of the alimentary canal.

Let's see what we can learn from another creepy crawly thing. Just as caterpillars are the larvae of butterflies, inchworms are the larvae of Geometer moths. Because inchworms don't have as many little feet as other kinds of caterpillars, they do the best they can with the legs they have, which are in front and in back. An inchworm grabs onto something in front of it, and then pushes its body upward into a shape much like an upside-down "U" until its back legs meet its front legs. Then it grabs on with its back legs and pushes forward to reach the next destination point, and repeats the process. This is just what an inchworm has to do to get where it's going. By moving this way, it looks like it is methodically measuring the ground over which it travels.

There is a Sesame Street song about an inchworm you may remember from when you were a kid. Most people remember the part that goes "Two and two are four; four and four are eight," and so on. But the important part for us, and the part that relates to the cocoon, is the other part of the song:

> Inch worm, inch worm
> Measuring the marigolds —
> You and your arithmetic
> You'll probably go far.
> Inch worm, inch worm
> Measuring the marigolds —
> Seems to me you'd stop and see
> How beautiful they are[viii].

Did you catch it? Do you see the problem that rarely, if ever, gets solved outside of the cocoon? Everyday life is too busy, too noisy, and too full of distractions. The inchworm seems to be so busy measuring its steps that it never looks at the beauty and wonder all around it. The take-away for us is that we can get so caught up in doing things that keep us busy and distracted, that we miss the really important aspects of living. There seems to be just a little too much noise and distraction in our lives to focus on reflection and evaluation. We need the cocoon to shut out the noise and distractions for a while, so we can complete the inside job on ourselves that's needed to undergo metamorphosis and move forward as people changed for the better.

Pointless busyness siphons off energy that can be better invested in our future growth. Sometimes we have responsibilities that cannot be put aside, but if we're honest, sometimes we get in the habit of being busy for the sake of being busy. It is a tactic for avoiding boredom or for escaping things we don't want to face.

Rocks and Tyrants

In the late 1960s, Charles Hummel used the phrase "the tyranny of the urgent" to describe our tendency to bow down to the things that scream for our immediate attention, even if other things, quieter things, have greater impact and true importance in our lives[ix]. The cocoon is the place where we make the tyrant sit down and shut up. We take the "rant" out of tyRANT.

There is also a story about a teacher who was trying to make a point about time management to a group of college students. You may have seen this story as it made its rounds on the Internet. The story also appeared in Stephen Covey's book *First Things First: To Live, to Love, to Learn, to Leave a Legacy*[x].

> A teacher brought a big, empty jar to class. First, he put a bunch of big rocks in the jar, until they reached the top.
> "Is the jar full?" he asked the class.
> "Yes!" came the reply.
> The teacher sprinkled pebbles into the jar, and they rolled down to fill in around the big rocks.
> "Is it full yet?" the teacher asked.
> "I think so," answered one student, hesitantly.
> The teacher poured sand into the jar and asked, "How about now?"
> The students had caught on and responded, "No! Not full yet!"
> Grinning, the teacher poured water over the sand until the water reached the very rim of the jar, and asked one last time, "Is it full?"
> "Yes!" the students shouted.
> Sitting on the edge of the desk next to the jar, the teacher looked at the eager faces before him and posed a final question.
> "What is the lesson here?"

Someone blurted, "No matter how much we have going on in our lives, we can always do more."

"No," said the teacher. "The lesson is that, if we don't put the big rocks in the jar first, they will never fit in the jar later on."

The cocoon is the place where we:

- Dump out the jar

- Wash it out

- Sort through what was in it, and

- Decide what to keep, what to add, and what to throw away

Most importantly, the cocoon is where we make sure that we know which rocks are the big rocks, and that we put the big rocks in the jar first.

Is This "Cocoon" Really Necessary?

In a word, yes. If you are reading this, it is probably not because you want everything in your life to stay exactly the way it is now, right? You want something different. Maybe you think you want a relationship with a different person. Maybe you want to keep your relationship with this person, but you don't want it to keep going the same way it's been going. Maybe you are not in a relationship now, but you want to be ready to consciously respond in different ways, better ways, healthier ways, the next time a relationship opens up before you. How do you get there from here?

You have to understand you can only work or do work on yourself and control what is yours to be controlled. Also, remember that your progress is not contingent upon your partner's participation or lack thereof. It's not someone else's job to grow with you. It's not your partner's job to change when you change. And your growth is not contingent upon any other human being's participation. You have to do it. It has to be about you when you're trying to let go. A lot of times we're holding onto the partner thinking:

> If you work with me to change, our relationship will get better.

> I'll change when you change.

> If you show me you're committed, then I'll show you I'm committed.

No, at the end of the day, relationships are, as I have said before, a classroom, and the curriculum is yours. If you want to become a better person in relationship, it is your responsibility to become a better person in life. This is how you evolve; this is how you move forward.

When you reflect the transformed person you've become after doing your homework in the cocoon, that reflection will attract better people and may even motivate the people around you to become better people, too. The other person is getting a reflection from you, and that person's job is to use the information received as input for his or her own re-contextualization. And guess what? Others do it at a different rate than you do. You do it at a different rate than they do. Your sister does it at a different rate than your mother. Your brother does it at a different rate than your father. It doesn't make sense to try to wait for someone else to evolve and grow and meet you at some idealized point of maturity or development, when you, and they, and everyone else are still in flux, each working on his or her own self-paced curriculum. So don't wait for your partner to match you. Don't sit back and think that your progress is contingent on someone else's progress, because it isn't. It is normal for people to move and change and grow at totally different rates.

37

Building Your Cocoon

What kind of cocoon do you need? As we have seen, transformation is most likely to occur in the context of a safe environment that promotes quiet reflection and preserves the emotional and spiritual energy needed for deep accountability-based introspection and self-awareness.

However, different people process differently. When you have to make a big decision, do you operate best by clearing the decks and immersing yourself in the decision-making process? Or do you prefer to chew on things bit by bit letting them percolate over time? Either way is fine, as long as you don't let other things get in the way of the "cocoon" time you need.

If you are comfortable with writing or journaling, it can be a great tool for processing your thoughts and feelings while recovering in the cocoon.

Anybody who has gone through any kind of difficult relationship can benefit from writing about it. It doesn't have to be an intimate relationship. It could be a business relationship. But it could be a marriage or even a traumatic parent/child relationship. Creative writing or expressive writing can be a way to understand what has been problematic and hurtful about the relationship. You don't have to show anyone else what you've written. It's not for them. It's your very own life sketchpad; it's for your eyes only, if you want it to be.

You might call it a release journal. The purpose of it is to reflect, vet, release, and —here's the key—re-contextualize your beliefs. When you re-contextualize your beliefs after you've gone through an experience, it is like the caterpillar digesting what it ate to pull out all of the nutrients. Yes, it may have tasted bad. Yes, it may have hurt. Yes, it may have made you more sensitive. But processing through the experience allows you to re-contextualize yourself in a way that encompasses the experience itself, as part of your transformation from who you are now to who you are becoming. The experience itself was hard, and thinking deeply about this ordeal and its past and future context is also difficult, maybe even harder than the experience itself. That's why it requires being closed off in a cocoon. But the payoff, the gain from all the pain, is that when you emerge from the cocoon, you are a new and more beautiful being.

You can postpone this process by avoiding the cocoon altogether, or you can hijack the process by choosing to stay in the cocoon when it is time to emerge and move forward. You have to take charge of how you respond to the pain. Let it drive you into the cocoon, but don't let it hold you back by distorting your perceptions or making your future moments slaves of your past experiences and memories. Obviously pain and hurt don't feel good, but when you invest time in the cocoon to glean every useful, nourishing thing out of experiences, good or bad, you can open up and blossom. You can become all that you were meant to be. And, as a bonus, changing yourself changes the equation. Your relationships and your world won't be the same when a different, better you surfaces from the cocoon of self-healing.

EXERCISE 3: PUTTING THESE IDEAS INTO PRACTICE

In the next few chapters, we will go into detail about what goes on in your cocoon, what steps to take and what things to ponder and evaluate there.

For now, take a minute to think about what you need to do to put the world on "pause" and create your transformation space.

In what kind of physical environment do I feel safe and able to focus?

_____

_____

What will I need to do to shut out noise and distractions?

_____

_____

When will I muster the courage to set my sacred appointment with myself in my "cocoon"?

_____

_____

What relationship or attitude will I work on during my "cocoon" time?

_____

_____

IN THE COCOON

Chapter 4

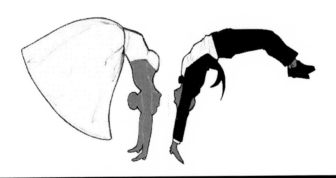

Self-Reflection and Self-Examination

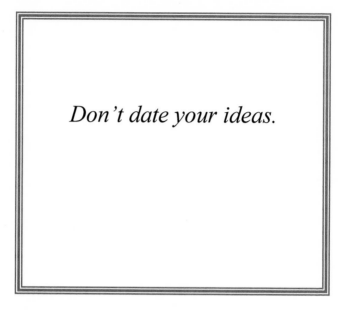

Don't date your ideas.

Start Right Where You Are

Are you frustrated with me yet? It probably seems like I'm telling you to get all analytical and cerebral when your emotions are raw and throbbing. Maybe you don't want to think about it or even feel it at all, anymore. Maybe you just want the pain to go away. There's a difference, though, between hiding or burying the pain, or pretending it's not there, and actually grieving the pain and processing through it.

I know you can't get to the intellectual stuff until you come to grips with the pain, so I'm not asking you to do anything but start wherever you are. That's the only place anyone can start any journey.

You have thoughts, feelings and memories of whatever relationship you decided to bring to the cocoon to work on. Imagine that those thoughts, feelings, and memories are a video recording. Plan to playback that video twice, at least, and maybe several times.

Maybe the first few playbacks are about sitting with the pain and grieving the situation. Then, later, play back that video with an eye toward analyzing it, evaluating your choices and responses, and using critical thinking to see where your beliefs, perspectives or assumptions were distorted.

Processing Involves a Process

Whether you have faced a serious hurt in a cornerstone or stepping-stone relationship, and you need to work through it so you can start moving your perspective of that relationship to a better place, or whether you are grieving the loss of a relationship that has died, there is no magic switch to flip to get over it, and move on. Moving on requires you to walk with and through the pain. It is a step-by-step process. These steps can be arranged in many diverse ways, and also common sense tells us that different people may experience and see the process in divergent ways or over different time frames. But there is a pattern, whether you look at it as a series of linear steps or as a cyclical progression, the underlying pattern still remains.

You may have heard about the stages of grief that Dr. Elizabeth Kübler-Ross described people having when they face death: denial, anger, bargaining, depression and acceptance[xi]. In a 2013 *Psychology Today* article, psychologist Jennifer Kromberg applies those stages to the break up of a relationship[xii]. It makes sense to do that, since a break up is a change in one's being and essence, like a death. The "we" has been obliterated, and the deeper and more intense the relationship was, the more devastating the ripping apart of one's identity when the relationship changes radically or ceases to exist. To the extent someone has started to define himself or herself in terms of that relationship, of being part of "we," there is a loss; a death of one's very concept of self. That is huge. If you try to sweep something that big under the rug and pretend it is not there, you will trip over it every time you try to move forward and land flat on your face.

You have to face it before you can get over it and move on. I learned one pattern for working through it from a source that may surprise you: the legendary Hip Hop artist Kool Mo Dee.

Kool Mo Dee's Four Cycles of a Break up

Starting with a chance encounter in 1997, I have developed a valuable friendship over the years with Hip Hop legend Kool Mo Dee. He was the catalyst for amplifying my understanding of my purpose, as well as persuading me to express the multitude of ideas and notions I had researched and developed from my life experiences and studies along my journey up to that point. Kool Mo Dee urged me to write my first self-published book *The Rebirth of Seeds*.

A lot of people don't know that Kool Mo Dee is a very deep, philosophical, spiritual and highly educated guy. They think he's just a rapper and wonder why anyone should take advice from an old school Hip Hop head. "Well, don't judge a book by its cover," I always say.

For more than ten years, Kool Mo Dee and I have done Relationship Roundtables all over the country—from New York to LA and everywhere in between. We've done them at clubs; we've done them in private homes; we've done them everywhere. Kool Mo Dee often suggests a four-month time frame of intense self-reflection to work through a bad break up.

I know that the time frame may vary, depending on the depth, duration and intensity of the relationship, and the personalities of the people involved, but the model and the pattern of cycles within it provides a useful framework for adjusting expectations about what it really means to "get over" a break up.

The first time he told me about the four-month time frame and the pattern of cycles in that time frame, it was about fourteen years ago, and I was going through another break up. I was a mess; I'll acknowledge it. Kool Mo Dee told me, "After a break up, in terms of time, it should be four months; break those four-month periods down into four 30-day cycles and then break those cycles into the four planes of consciousness."

Cycle 1: The first 30-day cycle is the **physical** separation. You broke up. You're not talking, and you're not seeing each other. During that first thirty days, you can expect to have physical withdrawal symptoms because, depending on how long you were together, there's a physical attachment on a biochemical level. That includes the sexual aspect, which is very significant, since sexual energy is also essentially spirit energy, which makes it hard to disconnect. Give yourself 30 days (at least) to focus, meditate, pray and cut spiritual cords on that plane. Of course, these phases are not linear and/or monolithic; they're phasing in and out at different times, but this is a starting point for where your focus should be.

Cycle 2: The next 30 days is the **emotional** phase. Through mediation and objective self-observation you'll be dealing with your feelings exclusively in this phase. You may be confronted by your anger, which is born of frustration, which is born from not getting what you want. You might be disappointed and you might have feelings of betrayal. This is normal. Hug them. Sit with these feelings, embrace this curriculum and don't run from or avoid what you feel. Give them a place in your home, treat them as an honored royal guest and then they will unravel and reveal the gift of closure. Closure, understanding and acceptance go hand in hand.

Cycle 3: The next 30-day phase is **mental**. When you enter this phase, you are starting to contextualize your beliefs and your philosophies about this relationship and the person. Now you have the opportunity to see them for who they really are. Maybe they've done things that you never thought they would do, and you're starting to see them behave in ways that make you go, "Wow, maybe I did not know this person at all." No, they're just showing another layer of themselves. They're simply showing who they are in a moment of conflict. They've always been that; it's just that there was no opportunity to see this aspect of that person until you got to this level of conflict that showed you how they would respond in the moment. So this mental phase requires that you use critical thinking skills to reorganize your thoughts and adapt your perspective. When new information is brought to the table, you ought to re-contextualize old beliefs; that's the mental portion.

Cycle 4: The fourth cycle, the last 30-day cycle, is the **spiritual**. This involves spiritual releasing, where forgiveness comes into play.

Maybe you need to go through this process twice a year; that means you spend eight months of the year in prayer/visioning, in spiritual work on yourself—in meditation, where you put yourself through the four phases of spiritual, physical, mental and emotional cleansing and releasing. Maybe this process will work for you; maybe it won't. Maybe you just need somebody to listen to you. Maybe you just need to listen, actively listen, to what is going on inside yourself.

But it is a definite recipe for disaster if you try to run into a new relationship and haven't done any of these things. It would be like a gymnast trying to mount up for a second vault without a clean dismount from the previous vault. An improper dismount impairs the gymnast. Landing wrong causes injuries. Why hobble stubbornly into the next launch, only to cause yourself further injury? Take time to land right, or if you already landed wrong, take time to heal from it.

Playback 1: Sit with the Pain

If you ever saw the Diana Ross movie, *Lady Sings the Blues*, then you probably heard a powerful song called "Good Morning, Heartache," made famous by the subject of the movie, the late, great jazz and blues singer Billie Holiday. This song captures the idea of sitting with the pain, and treating it as an honored guest. The lyrics to the song are:

> Good morning, heartache, you ole gloomy sight
> Good morning, heartache, thought we'd said goodbye last night
> I turned and tossed until it seemed you had gone
> But here you are with the dawn
> Wish I'd forget you
> but you're here to stay
> It seems I met you
> When my love went away
> Now every day I start by saying to you
> Good morning, heartache, what's new?
>
> Stop haunting me now
> Can't shake you, no how
> Just leave me alone
> I've got those Monday blues
> Straight through Sunday blues
>
> Good morning, heartache, here we go again
> Good morning, heartache, you're the one who knew me when
> Might as well get used to you hangin' around
> Good morning, heartache, sit down[xiii].

Once you get past acting like you have no need for the grieving process, you can start acknowledging what you really feel. According to Dr. Kübler-Ross' grief stages, anger is probably the next thing you will feel. You may be mad at your partner for

49

causing you grief or disappointment, or mad at yourself for accepting what you knew wasn't right, or consciously overlooking things that you knew weren't right in the relationship. You may have consciously ignored your intuition. It is at this stage that you are in the greatest danger of playing the blame game and casting yourself in the starring role of "victim." Feel it. Vent it. Journal it. Do what you need to do to sit with it, but keep moving through it.

Anger takes a lot of energy; so most people can't sustain anger forever. Eventually you'll move past being mad that you didn't get what you wanted from the relationship and start trying to get creative about how, just maybe, you can still engineer things to get what you want, after all. The danger of this phase is that, if you let it go unchecked, you can become a first class manipulator. This is the bargaining phase, where you think you are willing to promise anything, as long as you get what you want in return. In this phase, you are at risk of losing something even more important than your dignity – you may compromise your authenticity and ask your partner to do the same. It's like the child who pleads for the toy at the store. *"Pleeeeeease! If I can just have this, I'll never ask for anything else, ever again!"* That's the kind of promise you wouldn't dream of making, if your rational mind were online. But the bargaining phase of grief is about the rule of desires, not the rule of reason. This phase might look or sound a little bit like a real commitment to doing the hard, painful work that is required to reboot and restore a relationship, but the difference is that a real commitment is steady and unwavering, based on a reasoned decision and "spiritual conviction" that this is a cornerstone relationship worth pursuing, no matter how long it takes and no matter whether results or changes are slow in coming. The bargaining characteristic of this stage of grief is a shallow kind of wishful thinking that quickly falls by the wayside of life circumstances or the other person fails to deliver as expected.

The next stage is depression. It is a kind of bone-weariness and hopelessness that comes from realizing that it really is beyond your power to make things go your way. On the way to giving up the fantasy of having what you want, it can feel like you have just plain given up. It would feel like sorrow, if you weren't too tired and numb to feel much of anything, at this point. Life feels hard. Nothing seems interesting or worth the effort. This is a bleak place. Keep hanging in there. Things will get better. Some people need help getting through this phase, but it will eventually pass, like the other stages of grief.

Finally, there is acceptance. Acceptance is the last phase of grief that Dr. Kübler-Ross identifies. The odd thing about acceptance is that circumstances are usually no different than they were at the beginning of the spiritual ordeal commonly known as "relationship death (bad break up)." It's just that your perception of it all has changed.

In the song "Gotta Make It to Heaven," Multi-platinum rapper and businessman 50 Cent quotes a prayer that people learn in twelve-step programs. It's known as the Serenity Prayer and goes like this:

> Lord, grant me
> the serenity to accept the things I cannot change,
> the courage to change the things I can,
> and the wisdom to know the difference[xiv].

When the full force of the emotion is spent, and you can accept the things you cannot change, like circumstances and other people's choices, only then you are ready to be objective enough to do the analytical part: figuring out what you can and should change, and doing the hard work of changing it.

Playback 2: Ask Yourself the Hard Questions

On the second playback (or the second season of playback), it is time to take an honest look at the thoughts, behaviors, and events recorded in the "video" of memory. It takes strength and courage to look at what really happened and deal with it. When the pain and emotions are not distorting your perceptions, there is a better chance that you will see clearly enough to find answers to hard but revealing questions like:

Where did I blind myself?
Where did I filter out what I didn't want to see?
Where did I date an imbalanced idea?
Where did I deceive my partner?
Where did I demand that my unrealistic expectations be fulfilled?

Renouncing Blindness

Now that you are looking back at the relationship with some objectivity, can you see places where you were blinding yourself? Be honest. Where were you embracing denial, because it was easier than facing up to what was really happening? Later on, it will be important to think about where you may have deceived your partner, but you won't be able to recognize the times you did that if you don't first take off the blindfold and see where you were in denial and maybe were even deceiving yourself.

Dating the Real and Now – Not Ideas, the Past or Future

When you go into a relationship, you might think you are dating a real person. But play back the tape from the start of that relationship you are thinking about, and be honest about what you find. Did you see the person that was really there? Or did you see what you wanted to see, or what you expected to see?

We get into relationships with people who share similar ideas, and we believe that to be compatibility. It's not necessarily bad to have things in common, but if your ideas have never been challenged, how do they grow? What happens if you're just getting with somebody who thinks the same way as you but who doesn't behave the same way as you? You find yourself dating an idea and not a real person. I always tell people *"Don't date your ideas. Date a real person because that person, any person, is always in flux and always changing, and it is the difference and change that stretches you and makes you grow.*" I believe that true intelligence, and not just being book-smart or book-read, seeks to challenge itself. People who are intelligent, conscious and aware understand that challenge is a conduit to growth. Challenge doesn't always have to be argumentative, and it doesn't always have to be violent. But challenge may involve contrast or opposing views. A lot of people are uncomfortable having their beliefs challenged. Some people even think that anyone who disagrees with them is dissing them or rejecting them. The way disagreement is expressed can show disrespect or rejection, but disagreement can also be expressed respectfully. In fact, I may be doing you a disservice if I pretend to agree with you, when I really think something else. Not to express disagreement appropriately cheats you out of an opportunity to grow by thinking about the other side of the coin.

I believe that it's easy for most people to have a kind of extreme thought process in terms of their idea for happiness. When I say extreme, what I'm really saying is somewhat of an imbalanced perspective that only considers one side of the picture. It's like the difference between dreaming in stereo as opposed to dreaming in mono. Think about having your own home. Everybody dreams to have a home but nobody dreams to have it foreclosed. Nobody wishes for a second mortgage. Nobody dreams about termite infestation, or the home's upkeep. Nobody dreams about the responsibilities that come with having a home. We just dream about holidays, picnics and all of the other things we're going to do at the home.

Black and white thinking works the same way. Most people only think about things from their own beliefs and their own perspectives. But they don't recognize that those views are *their* beliefs and perspectives; instead, most people would say, *"This is the way things are."* Do you see the difference between saying, *"This is the way things are,"* and saying *"This is the way I see it"?* Saying *"This is the way things are"* makes it seem that I think my perspective is the only real, true or possible perspective. If I go into a relationship thinking like this, and the relationship environment does its natural work of challenging the imbalanced thought with a different or opposing idea, I am faced with a choice at the crossroads of that conflict. I can respond with flexible thinking, and test my idea to see if it is always true, sometimes true, or never true. I can see if there is a way to reconcile our ideas and make them fit together somehow. But I have to be open to change, to be able to respond that way. If I am rigid and inflexible in my thinking, then it is the inflexibility of my response and not the differences presented by the other person's ideas that creates the risk of shutting down the relationship. A lot of researchers will tell you that high-functioning relationships typically have flexible beliefs rather than black and white thinking. There may be some beliefs in your life that are bedrock beliefs, non-negotiable beliefs that define you, but most beliefs are more ambiguous. There is more gray area than there is black or white thinking in life. When you don't have any room for gray, and think that it is either this or that, and nothing in between, you're setting your relationship up to fail. Often we have to seek flexibility to find it. Even our beliefs need yoga. Even our beliefs need to learn how to stretch. Because a belief can either be a liberator that gives us the elasticity to bend and to grow, or a belief can harden into a prison; into a cage. Black and white thinking is one thing we do to turn a relationship into a prison as opposed to the Garden of Eden/Love, where things continuously grow.

Being Real

Do you remember how much it hurt the first time your partner did something totally unexpected? I don't mean, unexpected but fun like doing something spontaneous. I mean something that made you feel embarrassed or betrayed, and you thought, *"Who is this person? I don't know this person at all!"*

Well, guess what? Any time you pretend to be something you're not, you are setting your partner up to have that same experience.

Maybe you feel a little insecure, so you are trying to put on something that you think will be more impressive, or more powerful. Maybe you are really feeling hurt or humiliated, but you don't want to let it show, because you want to protect yourself or don't want to look weak. What you are really doing is building up a wall of deception between you and your partner. You've got to take off the mask of who you project yourself to be, and be the real you with your partner. Otherwise, bad things could happen, like having your partner fall in love with the façade, only to be disappointed when the real you appears, or like having your partner reject the fake you, without even having gotten to know the real you, which is the person that your partner might have truly loved.

My Way or the Highway

When I make demands that my partner must meet my expectations, it's like saying that, in our relationship, *"It's my way or the highway."* That expression usually means that you have to do things my way or clear out, or do things my way or I'm leaving. There's another way to look at the "highway," though, and that is as a "high" way that takes the high road. Instead of demanding my way, I can choose to take the high road of love.

What does the high road of love look like? There's a bible translation called *The Message* that puts it this way:

> Love never gives up.
> Love cares more for others than for self.
> Love doesn't want what it doesn't have.
> Love doesn't strut,
> Doesn't have a swelled head,
> Doesn't force itself on others,
> Isn't always "me first,"
> Doesn't fly off the handle,
> Doesn't keep score of the sins of others,
> Doesn't revel when others grovel,
> Takes pleasure in the flowering of truth,

Puts up with anything,
Trusts God always,
Always looks for the best,
Never looks back,
But keeps going to the end[xv].

EXERCISE 4: PUTTING THESE IDEAS INTO PRACTICE

Are you ready to take a cold, hard, objective look at that relationship? Take a minute to think about how the ideas in this chapter relate to your life and experiences.

Where did I blind myself in this relationship? Where did I filter out what I didn't want to see?

_____

_____

Where in this relationship was I really dating an imbalanced idea?

_____

_____

Where did I deceive my partner in this relationship?

_____

_____

Where in this relationship did I demand that my imbalanced expectations be fulfilled?

_____

_____

SELF-REFLECTION AND SELF-EXAMINATION

Chapter 5

Accountability | Letting Go of Blame and Powerlessness

> *Proper dismounts take hard work, self-examination, discipline and the courage to change*

You Are in Charge of Your Abilities

Many people hate feeling out of control. Sometimes a situation or a relationship feels bad enough by itself, but then when you add the terrible feeling that you can't do anything about the bad situation or relationship, it seems even worse. In most cases, though, powerlessness and victimhood are an illusion.

True, you may not be able, by yourself, to change the circumstances around you. You can invite or encourage the other person to change, but you certainly can't *make* anyone else change.

But you are in charge of your abilities – the things you are able to do:

- You can look at things realistically.

- You can take stock of the things you do that helped contribute to the situation or that helped corrupt the relationship.

- You can adopt new ways of thinking, being, doing, speaking, acting, and responding.

In other words, you can be accountable and responsible for your own stuff, no matter what the other person chooses to do or not do.

The Crossroads of Facing the Truth

Let's look again at Michael Jackson's words of musical wisdom: *"I'm starting with the man in the mirror[xvi]."* Why start there? The truth is, if you don't acknowledge the things you did that contributed to a relationship going sour, all you get is the pain with none of the gain. Facing the truth puts you at a crossroads. You can own your part of the problem, grow from it, and undergo transformation through it, or you can shift blame to others (at least, in your own mind – in reality, it always is what it *really* is) and stay stuck in a downward spiral. Let's look at two different paths available at this crossroads and consider the cost of each option.

Proper Dismounts and Improper Dismounts

In a gymnastics routine, a proper dismount brings closure to the routine. A good, or "stuck," landing is a stance of stability that is a strong takeoff point for the next routine. Every gymnast understands that with angular momentum, and with hours upon hours of practice and falling on the cushion that a proper dismount can be executed. When the lights come on, and it's time to perform, the trained gymnast knows how important every single aspect of the routine is, and no aspect is more important than the dismount. The dismount is the coup de grâce—the cherry on top. It is the exclamation point. I draw on this gymnastics metaphor for this book in terms of how to break up properly, and to show people how, metaphorically speaking, to "stick the landing." Sticking the landing simply means being able to move on into a new experience without the residue from the old. Landing well from a relationship means being able to emerge from the heartbreaking or painful experience of losing a loved one through break up as if one is emerging from a cocoon, transformed into a new being—a better being than the one who just went through the drama, failure or trauma that came from your last relationship routine. This metamorphosis lets one walk away with more knowledge of oneself and more awareness of one's own effect on the relationship. Taking responsibility for discovering and acting on these insights makes it possible to move forward without the residue of resentment, hurt, betrayal, anger and frustration that so often accompanies a break up, whether it's a gradual break up or a sudden one.

Think for a minute about a gymnast who lands with a 25-pound weight dangling from one shoulder. That mental image might make us wonder how the weight got there, but there is another question that is more important. How can the gymnast remove that weight and put it down, so that the weight does not keep dragging her off balance in this routine and in every future routine?

Closure in a relationship means that it is finished; it is released. All the weights that threaten to throw us off balance, and all of the relationship debris that we might be tempted to carry into the next relationship, will either be removed or they will weigh us down and limit our ability to soar into future relationships.

Proper dismounts take hard work, self-examination, discipline and the courage to change. A proper dismount in a relationship happens at the right time, after hard work and self-examination. It brings growth and closure. As far as possible, it sets both parties up for more satisfaction in future relationships, without bitterness or regret.

Contrast the proper dismount with an improper dismount, or a premature dismount, which is almost like a gymnast not finishing the routine. How many of us carry baggage? We call it emotional baggage. We carry baggage of unresolved relationship issues from one relationship to the next. We assume that we're okay, and that the problem was because of the other person, or that the problem was there were too many differences and disconnects with the other person. So we conclude that the next relationship will be better, if we just choose a partner whose belief system is more closely aligned with our own. And by "belief system," I don't just mean spiritual or religious beliefs. I am talking broadly about all the assumptions we make about everything, including about how life works, values, priorities, expectations and perspectives. But belief systems require examination, as author and speaker Robert Anton Wilson pointed out when he said, *"...Once you have a belief system everything that comes in either gets ignored if it doesn't fit the belief system, or it gets distorted enough so that it can fit into the belief system. You've got to be continuously revising your map of the world*[xvii]*."* We make a mistake if we expect a relationship to provide a safe haven for our existing belief systems, when, in actuality, the relationship is where our belief systems get challenged the most.

That's why a dismount—a proper dismount—is being able to see the reflections that are coming back to you from the relationship as curriculum for oneself. When you see these reflections/bio-feedback, they have often been called red flags/sign-posts for the things that you need to work on. These triggers are the reflections that are coming back to you from your partner that you may have not known about yourself. For example, why is it that I'm more impatient about listening to my partner than I am with other people? Why am I more patient when I am listening to casual acquaintances or to strangers?

I think we get what I call premature dismounts because things don't feel right or things don't feel good. I have to let people know that the whole purpose of letting go and releasing in the course of making a proper dismount is to free you from carrying relationship debris into your next intimate experience. The dismount is synonymous with closure, which is synonymous with understanding. And most of us don't have a sufficient level of understanding to bring closure to the myriad relationships we've been through. And we don't have a philosophy in general that says relationship is a hospital for souls, so we rarely expect to engage in the kind of self-reflective exercises that promote healing and growth, which are necessary to achieve a proper dismount *(i.e., closure)*.

How we get there is to acknowledge that no one is perfect and that every relationship you've ever been in has something to teach you. And if you accept the lesson/reflection about you as opposed to saying, *"It's their fault,"* otherwise known as "blaming," then you'll understand how to properly dismount and stick the landing when it's time for the relationship end. In my opinion, the proper method of breaking up, the proper method of releasing, has to do with accountability—personal accountability—the acknowledgment of what you brought to the table in terms of conflict, in terms of unconscious, unresolved issues. And once you get to the point where you can identify your contribution to where the relationship broke down, then you can stick the landing.

How Does an Improper Dismount Make You Stumble into Your Future?

Many people try to enter a new relationship too soon. I don't just mean that they rush into a new relationship or a rebound relationship too soon in terms of time alone. For me, the real problem arises when entering a relationship too soon in terms of fragmented processing. Time without processing is just waiting; it's not healing. To put it more bluntly, the typical person does little processing other than to feel angry or sad for a while. Once the pain recedes a little, or maybe to escape the pain, the person starts wondering how to get back into the relationship game. I do offer some tips about that, but first things first.

If you seek to start a new relationship after you've gone through a tumultuous break up, and you carry into that new relationship resentment, fear, anger or frustration, you will be entering a rebound relationship instead of a true relationship, and all the emotional baggage you carry into the new relationship will corrupt it. It's like flunking a class. You automatically get re-enrolled. Relationship breakdown can bring pain and panic, as if life is falling apart, but in reality, hitting hard times and bumps in the road are part and parcel to being a human being. It's part of the human condition. The pain is a sign that it is time to go into labor, so that a better you, who can be ready to engage in a better relationship, can be born. To go into a new relationship with old, unresolved issues poisons the new relationship, thereby limiting the potentiality of the relationship to become the one you so desire. A rebound relationship is a stillborn relationship at worst; at best, it is a relationship with its growth stunted from the beginning.

A rebound relationship is like watching a horror movie over and over again with only one difference. Each time you watch it, it's got new people in it, or a new cast of characters. A rebound relationship is Spiritual Arrested Development (SAD) because what you're doing is wearing a mask and saying, *"Oh, this is okay. I'm over it."* We live in the "I'm Over It" culture, trying to convince ourselves by saying statements like, *"Oh, I'm done. I'm through. I'm over it."* No, you're not! Too often, we're just moving on because we know if we don't move on, life is going to drag us forward, anyway. But people try to move on superficially, without really taking inventory of what needs to be dealt with. A woman might change boyfriends like she changes underwear. A man might change girlfriends like he changes the oil in his car. It seems like a new situation, with some new scenery. But beyond the façade of newness and the spray-on new car smell, it is really the same old same old.

Are you doing the same things that you did with the other person (the one you still haven't resolved your issues with)? Are you watching the same TV shows, eating the same meals or going out to the same movie theater? Do you find yourself going to the same restaurants you used to go to with your old love? Even though you've got a new person with you, are you still the same person you were when you were in your last relationship? Do you have the foolish expectation that this one relationship will work without you addressing you? *#commondenominator*

One of the major lessons that has to be learned is that you can never avoid the pain of dealing with the ordeal of you. You can mask it, or you can compartmentalize it, or you can deny it by not dealing with it. But it will be an unwelcomed impediment in your life until you address it. Its influence and effect will effectively mold and shape your relationships, whether you want it to or not.

You may remember hearing about a very visible disruption in the relationship of two celebrities, Chad Johnson (known for awhile as Chad Ochocinco) and his then-wife Evelyn Lozada. Even though their disruption became public, she did something that I considered to be of high moral and spiritual quality. She posted on her website a letter that she wrote to the 7-year-old version of herself, and in the letter she took steps to acknowledge that she was at the root of the drama and chaos that was swirling around her life. Evelyn Lozada gets my total respect because she acknowledged the hurt inner child that most people are afraid to address.

If you do not address the root causes of your disappointment, pain, anger or fear, you are doomed to carry the residue from unresolved experiences into a rebound relationship routine, and it may drain your energy and power. I think women are absolutely the most powerful human beings on planet Earth when they engage in personal accountability. When women fall into the societal construct of the "damsel in distress," the built-in victim, that's when women marginalize their own internal power.

When Evelyn Lozada became personally accountable for the drama she had magnetized into her life, it seems to me that she evolved spiritually. She rose up, because to acknowledge that you are the co-creator of the mess you're relating to is power. In the acknowledgment of your imperfection, you are now finding something that most people don't understand: perfection contains imperfection. That's balance, like in the metaphor of the yin and yang. Half of the yin is white, half of the yang is black and there's a dot of white in the black and there is a dot of black in the white. This presents a picture of wholeness or perfection.

I know I am getting closer to a state of perfection or balance when I can acknowledge that going through this situation prepared me to become a better person, and I had to go through it regardless of the extent of the pain, regardless of the intensity of the betrayal, regardless of what has happened. When I embrace the experience, including my faulty beliefs and expectations as well as my poorly chosen words and deeds, this is an opportunity for personal growth.

In a conversation I had with a former girlfriend who I had dated over 20 years ago, she told me that she felt she could be much more candid and open with me than she could be with her own husband. As we talked, she admitted that she had gone into the new relationship with her husband only a couple weeks after we broke up. She had been in a rebound relationship for over 20 years, and the repercussions of failing to properly dismount from the relationship that she and I had were still affecting her to this day.

In our zeal to run toward something better, we have to remember that we cannot run from ourselves. No matter where you go, there you are.

Short-Cuts That Short Circuit Your Growth

Casting blame on the other person is very tempting when you feel hurt or betrayed. *"You know what? It's his loss and I'm the victim, and I have no personal accountability in the way things unraveled. It was all on him."*

The problem with blaming someone else is that it takes the focus off of you and makes you see yourself as a victim who has neither power nor responsibility or choice. That's not a recipe for sticking the landing. That's a recipe for staying stuck in the same bad relationship patterns/routines over and over again.

You have a different option available to you. You can sit there and process the hurt or betrayal, asking questions like:

> *Why (for what purpose) did I go through what I went through?*

> *How does what I went through make me a better person?*

> *Where is the silver lining (personal accountability) in this situation that exonerates me from the victim role?*

People shouldn't need to find a villain or a scapegoat to take the blame for every bad, painful, disappointing experience. Accountability and responsibility are not about blame, shame, or fault. They are about empowerment to see what is really there and to change the things that are in your power to change.

When I ask people to take personal accountability—to be accountable for what they've experienced, I'll say, *"Give me an example of the negativity you contributed to the situation?"* And they will often say, *"Well, I was too nice."* That's not taking "freaking" personal accountability. Taking personal responsibility means acknowledging that part of what happened to me happened because of me. Look for that.

Saying *"My contribution to the problem is that I was too nice"* hides the real issues by sugarcoating them. It may be more accurate to say, *"I knew he was bad for me, but I went into the relationship anyway. And then I enabled him and made excuses for him.*" There is a difference between being "nice" and "enabling bad behavior (in yourself or in other people)."

I was talking to a young lady the other day about her fear of being in a relationship. She said, *"I want to be in a relationship but I'm afraid to be in one because I've been hurt so many times."* I said, *"Well, hurt is part of the movement but what have you learned from that movement? Has the hurt caused you to isolate and insulate yourself from the interaction you so desire?"* I said, *"If you desire this interaction but you're also building a wall around yourself, is that not a contradiction? How are you going to get over, through or under this wall? Do you build a door? Can people open the door and come in? Because you're going to have to let somebody come in."*

Far too often we live this contradictory, fragmented kind of life because we haven't reconciled pain; we haven't reconciled hurt. Some people think they reconcile hurt by saying, *"It's your fault."*

Another common response to pain is avoidance. So many people choose to live an empty existence and bounce from situation to situation just so they can feel something other than the pain. They will self-medicate with strobe lights from the nightclub, with high-end vodka, marijuana, sex, entertainment, work or anything else they can get their hands on, in order to avoid themselves in the moment of strife.

Some people go to church or meditate, but it's all superficial. They're not participating in these activities to understand their pain. They're doing it to feel better, and you can't self-medicate with platitudes like *"Everything's going to be okay. This is all for my highest good."*

Let me tell you something about the highest good—the highest good doesn't always feel good. And so many people get in the way of their highest good being delivered to them because they're under the illusion that they can control it. They wear a mask that says, *"This didn't affect me. I'm able to pick up and move on,"* instead of being authentic and acknowledging the hurt and impact. You can short circuit your own growth if you let the image you project out to other people be more important than who you really are.

If you don't want anyone to see you hurt, you might try the escape route of wearing a mask to present the image that people expect you to have. But that sacrifices the real you, and the better person you might become, for the sake of appearances that are not real. Instead of giving yourself a chance to dismount cleanly and stick the landing, you resort to spin tactics and try to edit the film so it looks like you did the internal work. But the people that were there saw the real performance, and in the end, masks and denial don't really fool anyone. They just delay healing and growth.

Most people feel comfortable living behind a mask. Why? Because they believe that ignorance is bliss. No one else knows what I'm going through because I'm behind this mask. Sometimes the experience will teach you what you don't know, and that dispels ignorance, in this context I'm saying ignorance is merely a lack of knowledge. Sometimes, though, ignorance involves a willful refusal to acknowledge what you do or should know. That kind of ignorance is consciously choosing to ignore what you know to be true about the person behind the mask. If you know that you still love someone, and you ignore that and move into another relationship, you're being stupid and ignorant, and you're arresting your own development. Self-examination may lead you to stay in the current relationship and transform it, or it may lead you to reconcile your ongoing love for the person with a conviction that a break up is necessary. Ignorance tends to lead people to do the wrong thing at the wrong time, for the wrong reasons.

Break ups help you come face-to-face with the darkest, deepest recesses of your own being, and that is where the real reconciliation is supposed to take place. Reconciling your weaknesses help you to become stronger in your next relationship.

You become more useful to your partner. You become more useful to yourself. You become a conduit of happiness. But you cannot become this conduit if you are afraid to deal with the things you are unhappy with. The answer to happiness is not an external one. It is an internal one. To dismount properly and stick the landing, we have to jettison silly little beliefs out there like: *"If I give him the best sex he's ever had, he'll never cheat on me,"* or *"If I provide her with everything she needs materially, she'll never leave me."* Relationships cannot be made secure by manipulating them with our good intentions or flawless performance. Secure, fulfilling relationships happen between people who are willing to own their own imperfections and strive to change them. Personal accountability is the key.

EXERCISE 5: PUTTING THESE IDEAS INTO PRACTICE

Think about how the ideas in this chapter relate to your life and experiences.

With a particular relationship in mind, ask yourself the following questions:

What emotional baggage (relationship debris) did I carry into this relationship?

_____

_____

What baggage/debris from unrealistic expectations or beliefs did I carry into this relationship?

_____

_____

How did that baggage/debris throw my perceptions and responses off balance?

_____

_____

What baggage/debris do I need to put down before I can soar freely into the next relationship (or the next phase of this relationship)?

_____

_____

THE RELATIONSHIP DISMOUNT

Chapter 6

Forgiveness | Letting Go of Shame and Guilt

> *When negativity gains momentum [and strength] in our relationship, it begins to mold reality, much like gravity bends light.*

What Is Forgiveness, Really?

Forgiveness as a term is believed to be disarming. In general, it is thought that when we forgive, we are to lay down our weapons. It is also believed that forgiveness allots us the necessary power needed to stop beating ourselves up and other people. To say, "I forgive you," means that there was an offense to pardon. It is an acknowledgment of a rift in the relational continuum, and it demands that I overcome the ignorance or denial of that fact. In the same breath, it is an outpouring of the healing balm of the grace and mercy that binds up the wound that it just identified.

In his book *The Peacemaker*, Ken Sande points out that forgiveness does not mean that you are excusing or forgetting about the offense, but rather that you are making a choice, perhaps repeatedly, whenever the offense comes to mind, to replace negative thoughts and feelings with positive ones[xviii]. That way, you don't keep reliving the offense and stumbling over it every time you think about it, and you are less likely to let it create a barrier between you and the offender. An illustration in the kids' version of the same book, *The Young Peacemaker*, shows the offended person helping the offender take off a T-shirt labeling him with the offense and put on a different T-shirt that says, "I am forgiven." This picture shows how the status, identity, and "label" of the offender changes whens the offended person forgives the transgressor for the offense[xix].

We sometimes hear about forgiveness in the financial world, too. Loan forgiveness cancels an outstanding debt, even though it was a valid obligation.   Some insurance companies offer "accident forgiveness," meaning that premiums won't go up, even though the insurance company might otherwise be able to justify a premium increase because the insured person was involved in an accident. These examples show us the side of forgiveness that involves releasing people from a burden or from otherwise just and understandable consequences of their actions and choices.

It is the same way when we forgive people who have hurt us, betrayed us, or disappointed us. There is a release *from* something, and perhaps more importantly, there is a release *to* something.

The Power of Forgiving Oneself

"I'll never forgive myself." Many of us have said or thought that at some point in life. But what does that mean? What are the implications of making a statement like that? Maybe we just intend to say that our pain, sorrow, or regret is so deep that we cannot imagine moving beyond them. But what may start as an anguished cry may become a habit of thinking that becomes a prison of our own making.

Should we feel pain? Yes. Should we grieve loss? Yes. Should we learn from bad experiences? Absolutely. But then we must move forward from that place of pain and grief. The point of owning our part of the problem and taking responsibility is to help us change and grow, not to punish ourselves and drown ourselves in regret until we wither and die.

Refusing to forgive ourselves can be a product of shame ("I'm so horrible I don't deserve forgiveness.") or from pride ("I'm smart enough to have known better, so I will demonstrate my superiority by withholding forgiveness from myself until I have flogged myself to my satisfaction."). It matters little which attitude is the source, since it produces a toxic, crippling result either way.

Forgiving oneself provides clemency from the merciless "inner warden" of shame and self-punishment for the mistakes of the past, and releases a person to soar into the future without ongoing regret and self-doubt.

The Power of Forgiving Others

The fact that someone is facing the question of forgiving someone else means that that person has been in pain, having been hurt or betrayed by the other. Depending on the extent of the hurt, pain, or betrayal, the natural response for most people is to want vengeance, justice or payback, or at least, harshly-delivered justice for the other person. Rarely do people feel like forgiving someone who has hurt them; instead, forgiveness usually involves an intentional choice, often in reliance on a higher power. Various religious traditions have a very high regard for forgiveness. One might even say forgiveness God's way of evolving the human heart to its highest level. This principle appears in many philosophical and religious teachings. The Buddha said, *"In order to understand everything one must forgive everything."* Jesus said, *"He who is forgiven little loves little (Luke 7:47 ESV[xx])."* There is a connection between forgiveness and understanding and a connection between forgiveness and love. The person who has been hurt risks being stuck in bitterness and resentment that will color future perceptions, warp future relationships and stunt future growth, unless that person chooses to stop following the *lex talionis,* the eye-for-an-eye principle that says, *"If you hurt me, I'm entitled to hurt you back. If you do me wrong, I'm going to do you wrong."* This is why I feel forgiveness is so difficult for so many. It is because of our inflexible desire for/pursuit of justified retribution that can potentially make us weak. Mahatma Gandhi once said, *"The weak can never forgive. Forgiveness is the attribute of the strong[xxi]."* It takes a tremendous about of internal fortitude to say, *"I no longer desire to pay you back."*

We must also be clear about what kind of forgiveness brings freedom. In my opinion, forgiveness has to be unconditional. If what we are labeling "forgiveness" is being treated as a tool of control/manipulation, reflecting anger, resentment and revenge, it is more like a truce or a cease-fire that lasts only as long as certain conditions are met. It is like loaning out mercy or forgiveness, based on an ultimatum.

Suppose you say, *"I will forgive you if you change your behavior. I will forgive you only if you promise to not do this or not do that or begin to do this or that."* What happens then? The other person is still not free, because there are still demands to be fulfilled. The offended person is still carrying the burden of remembering the original offense, as well as the new burden of policing and enforcing the conditional terms of the cease-fire. In some instances, these conditions are useful for the development of the relationship, but they must have an expiration date. Say for instance, if a partner has cheated, there must be some conditions in place that will demonstrate to the offended person that you are sincere about making a change for the better. But those conditions must operate like training wheels that are to be taken off at some point in the foreseeable future.

Even if the offender's behavior changes, there is no way to know whether the changed behavior came from insight and growth leading to a transformed heart and mind, or whether it is just a grudging response out of spousal duress or guilt, to get the offended person off his or her back. That kind of "forgiveness" does not restore anything or bring anything to closure. It is not real forgiveness. It is a tool of control or a guilt-trip masquerading as forgiveness.

I believe that true forgiveness objectively lays the whole mess down. Far from saying that there was no problem or that no one did anything wrong saying, *"I forgive you"* signals that a wrong was done, that a debt was incurred that requires repayment. And real forgiveness picks up a pen and writes across the face of that debt, "Paid in full." No more collection calls to make or receive. Forgiveness gives both people – the offender and the offended – a chance to have a new identity that is not defined by the offense.

Forgiveness is not just for the person that you're forgiving. Forgiveness is for the person who is doing the forgiving. You cannot dismount properly without forgiveness. Just as a highly trained athlete has to stop dwelling on past mistakes and past injuries to be able to let go of the fear of flying blind and to stick the landing to find success in the current routine and in subsequent routines, we need to do the same thing in relationships by letting go of the pain, bitterness and resentment by way of real forgiveness.

When I talk about closure and understanding, the clean dismount and the stuck landing, I am talking about the same thing. Closure means understanding that I can only control me. I understand that I can only take responsibility for what I do. I understand that forgiveness is more about elevating my soul than it is about exonerating another person. When that understanding is in place, a proper dismount is possible. Only then can I move forward without all of the relationship residue and debris from the unresolved past.

Forgiving Increases the Value of the Forgiven and the Forgiver

Forgiveness is costly, no matter how you look at it. If you see forgiveness as releasing a debt that someone else owes you, then forgiveness costs you the right to go back to the person and say,

"Hey, you owe me this." You could also see forgiveness as taking responsibility yourself for the cost of fixing what someone else broke. Maybe you loaned your car to a friend and he got into a fender bender. Or maybe you let somebody use your Xbox and he broke it. You might be able to expect, as a matter of justice, to have the person who did the damage make it right, and pay to fix or replace what was broken. However, relationship forgiveness is not as cut and dry. Relationship forgiveness is not solely about justice and retribution and making the other person pay. Forgiveness is about mercy (withholding the sometimes harsh outcomes that justice requires) and grace (offering good things that the other person has not "earned" or may not "deserve").

When you go beyond mercy to grace, you are talking about adding value to the thing that was broken within you and within the relationship. In that way, real, deep, true forgiveness in a relationship makes the union more valuable because of the cost of what has been invested to repair it.

There is a Japanese art form called *kintsukuroi* that involves mending broken ceramics with lacquer mixed with gold. This kind of repair does not try to hide the fact that the ceramic piece, such as a bowl or teapot, was dropped and broken. Instead, it makes the brokenness part of the item's new identity. But the repair is not done cheaply or carelessly. It is not just a matter of using metal staples for functionality to hold the parts together, like the ugly zig-zags of stitches holding the Frankenstein monster's head onto its body. *Kinsukuroi* is itself an art that embodies a philosophy[3].

---

[3] *For more about the richness of meaning embodied in kintsukuroi, see the essays in the exhibition booklet entitled FlickWerk: The Aesthetics of Mended Japanese Ceramics* at http://www.bachmanneckenstein.com/downloads/Flickwerk_The_Aesthetics_of_M ended_Japanese_Ceramics.pdf

The philosophy says that you don't just throw something away, especially if it has been meaningful to you. You take the time to lavish care and cost to heal it and restore it to usefulness and beauty. Using lacquer mixed with gold to hold the broken pieces of ceramic pottery together is expensive, because gold is an extremely rare material, and it requires skill to apply properly. But the resulting pattern of golden veins is even more beautiful than the original unbroken piece. In other words the overcoming of relationship trauma and brokenness can lead you to becoming more beautiful than you were before the transgression. One could say that the cracks in your relationship teapot were already there. You just needed the relationship to elucidate those cracks. This is the secret to what true forgiveness can offer to your soul; love, compassion and grace.

When I forgive someone who has hurt me in a relationship, I am not pretending that the hurt never happened. Instead, I am tracing the edges of all the broken places in the lavish relational gold of love, grace and forgiveness. I am making that relationship a vessel that is forever after stronger, more beautiful and precious to me than it was before. This is true, whether I put it on a shelf and look at it from time to time (as when I move on to a different relationship) or whether I continue to use it every day (as when I decide to stay in the relationship after my partner and I have chosen to repair it).

Without Forgiveness, Distorted Perception Can Lead to Destructive Responses

As we will discuss more fully in the final chapter, failing to forgive one's self can lead to crippling regret. Unforgiveness holds a person in bondage to resentment and fear, which can function as a distorted lens through which one views the world.

When we dwell on the wrongs done to us by focusing on the negatives – what we are afraid will happen or what is wrong with our relationship – we empower and give the negativity momentum and strength. When negativity gains momentum [and strength] in our relationship, it begins to mold reality, much like gravity bends light. One's perceived feeling of danger or failure can [warp and] distort current and future relationships. Left unchecked, the self-fulfilling prophecy of distorted perceptions and expectations can ultimately destroy relationships and alter one's sense of self.

When we see and expect only the bad, we are missing part of the truth of reality, because the bad never completely obliterates the good that exists. The bad just hijacks our focus, so we stop seeing the good.

There is a story circulating on the Internet that has appeared on various blogs and even in a few inspirational books. One version goes like this:

> A beautiful legend tells of an African tribe that ritualizes forgiveness. When a tribe member acts irresponsibly or unjustly, he/she is taken to the center of the village. All work ceases and every man, woman and child in the village gathers in a large circle around the accused. Then the tribe bombards the rejected person with affirmations! One at a time, friends and family enumerate all the good the individual has done. Every incident, every experience that can be recalled with some detail and accuracy is recounted. All their positive attributes, strengths and kindnesses are recited carefully and at length. Finally, the tribal circle is broken, a joyous celebration takes place, and the outcast is welcomed back into the tribe[xxii].

The kind of forgiveness shown in that ritual involves making an active effort to overcome distorted perceptions that may have proceeded from some transgression, by remembering the good that might otherwise be forgotten, and to use the affirmation of the good as a lens or filter for looking at the offender's identity. From that perspective, bitterness, resentment and regret lose their power to cripple, enslave and destroy. Hope is restored as the group moves together into the future.

A Letter for My Father (A Personal Application of Forgiveness)

For too many years, I have carried around anger, bitterness, and unforgiveness toward my father, James Gus Lewis. I realize that it is time to move past those feelings and replace them with an attitude of gratitude, grace, and love. If I could give my father a letter, it would say something like this:

> *First and foremost, let me say that I am thankful, and extremely appreciative for your help in giving me life, James Gus Lewis. I was too young to really understand the nature of your relationship with my mother, and with my older brothers and sisters. I don't need to find out the details about what happened between you and my family. I'm here to say simply that I love you and I forgive you, and myself, for every trespass, hurt, harm, and emotional and/or physical trauma that you committed against [them].*

> *I have often wondered what vaulted trajectory my life would have taken had you been more participatory during my maturation. I do recognize that I have many awesome gifts, and yet I also realize that your absence in my life has been to me like a curse, which has delayed the full development of my character. Still, I hold nothing against you, and I appreciate the limited time we had to spend with each other. You would think our spending such a small amount of time together would leave very little impact or resonance with me, but I'm here to tell you that even though we*

84

shared only a minute amount of time together, that time had the strength of a mustard seed and left an amazingly indelible impression on me.

I love you, James Gus Lewis. I release you of all resentment, hurt, disappointment, sadness, longing, and frustration that I have built up against you, others, and myself over the years. I release you from any responsibility associated with my failed relationships.

I love you, James Gus Lewis. I appreciate you, James Gus Lewis. And I still need you, James Gus Lewis.

Love and respect from your loving son,
Renard Williams, aka Zo Williams

For me, healing and closure came with reaching the point where my thoughts and feelings produced the words in this letter. Thinking, speaking, or writing words of forgiveness will not free you, unless they reflect the reality of forgiveness that has already happened in your heart and mind.

Sticking the landing in this way does not depend on the other person's response, so I can find freedom and a sense of peace, even if it is impossible for me to communicate forgiveness (for example, if the other person is deceased, or if I don't know where the other person is) or if it is unwise for me to communicate forgiveness (such as in abusive or violent situations in which direct communication could endanger my life). Receiving forgiveness can be a tremendous source of healing and blessing to the other person, too, once the other person recognizes that they have wronged you in a way that needs forgiving and feels remorse or sorrow for doing so.

EXERCISE 6: PUTTING THESE IDEAS INTO PRACTICE

This is a challenging topic, so I went first, to show you how to apply these ideas. You can see in my letter to my father how I might forgive unconditionally, no matter whether my father ever knows or responds in any way.

Please reflect on the following questions as you consider how the ideas in this chapter relate to your life and experiences.

Did you ever do something that you thought was unforgiveable? If so, what would it mean to you – and to the way you think about yourself, others, and your future – if you were to know that you were completely and unconditionally forgiven for whatever it was?

_____

_____

What do you need to release by receiving forgiveness, from God, from someone else, or from yourself?

_____

_____

What do you need to release by forgiving someone else?

_____

_____

What, if anything, is making it hard for you to forgive? What can you do to move past that obstacle?

_____

_____

When you have reached the reality of forgiveness in your heart and mind, write out your words of forgiveness in a journal or in a letter. Would it be wiser to keep this writing private? If so, why? Or should you share your forgiveness with the person you forgave, and if so, when, where, and how?

_____

_____

Chapter 7

Landing Well | Shedding Regret

> *Gotta let go of the guilt*
> *Gotta let go of the shame*
> *Gotta let go of regret*
> *Gotta let go of the blame*
> *Gotta let go of it all*
> *Before I get back in the game*
> *And when I let go*
> *I know*
> *That I*
> *Can finally fly*

Sticking the Landing

In Chapter 5, we talked about how important accountability is and how personal responsibility is essential to landing well from a relationship. Landing well means:

the routine is complete;

there is a proper dismount;

there is the best chance of avoiding injury; and

there is no unsteadiness or wobbling

Landing well puts you in the best position for the next takeoff, while landing badly leaves you hobbling into the future.

In the last chapter, we saw how vital forgiveness is to landing well and to bringing closure to the past, so that it is possible to move forward in freedom.

Now let's take a look at how to secure that freedom and keep it from getting hijacked by fear, pride, entitlement or regret.

Who or What is your Vizier?

"Vizier?" you might ask. "What is a vizier? Do I have one? Should I have one?"

In Muslim countries, the title of vizier (sometimes spelled as "wazir" or in other ways) is held by a minister of the government. The vizier may be, functionally speaking, the chief executive, or at least, the main face of ruling power that the subjects see. Throughout history, there have no doubt been some power-hungry viziers, whose behavior has fueled the stereotype of the untrustworthy advisor who manipulates the rightful ruler into doing his bidding or granting him riches, power, and favors. For example, think of the character of Jafar in the Walt Disney movie *Aladdin*, or of Haman manipulating the Persian King Xerxes in the biblical book of Esther.

The most effective power-snatching viziers (and that is not a compliment) are subtle enough to escape detection while they set the agenda and serve their own purposes in the course of their "advisory" duties. Most people succumb to the deception of a very crafty vizier/puppet master I call "FEGO."

"FEGO" is fear + ego. It is a potent mixture of fear and pride that slips in to distort our perception, take reason offline, and hijack every thought, word, and action to serve its own agenda. FEGO hates self-examination, because honest self-assessment is like turning on a floodlight, which dispels the shadows, making it difficult to hide.

FEGO's fear dimension debilitates our ability to move forward by encouraging us to hold onto regret and pain, which actually transforms every new situation into the old one. We fear getting hurt again if we forgive, if we release the relationship residue from all of the unresolved relationship debris from the past. So out of fear, we tend to surrender our power and give past resentments a strong advisory position in our future relationships. FEGO's ego dimension puts on a tough image and says, *"I've got it all together and I've moved on. I have to be strong, move on and show people that this didn't affect me."*

Ego makes us extremely superficial, so we delude ourselves into thinking that superficial change is real change. We are like set designers, changing the scenery but acting out the same script over and over again. The scenery is on the surface; the essence is within. You can change the scenery all day long and the essence remains. You must change the essence before external changes of appearance have any significance. When it comes to intimate relationships, most of us just change the set or cast a replacement for a vacant role, without evaluating and editing the script. In so doing we miss the point that every struggle and every pain offers the gift of growth and transformation to those who are willing to apply the new information that comes from objective observation.

Regrets, when we hold onto them, serve as a kind of time machine that transports the past into the present and empowers the past to mold and shape the present. This is why we get in trouble. This is how we can turn a new relationship into an old relationship with new people in it.

FEGO wants to keep us blind to the growth potential inherent in the breakdown of a relationship, so that we miss the valuable part of relational conflict and strife, which is to reconstruct us and rebuild us as new persons. Refusing to engage in objective self-evaluation and refusing to take appropriate responsibility for co-creating our painful experiences (or at least, for making our pain worse by the responses we choose) means that regret will forever be your companion and adviser.

Regrets, when we hold onto them, serve as a kind of time machine that transports us not back to the past but transports the past into the present and it puts it into the present in a creative sense because now the past is molding the present. This is why we get in trouble. This is how we can turn a new relationship into an old relationship with new people in it.

FEGO is an untrustworthy adviser. FEGO is a rotten vizier for anyone's life. It is time to fire FEGO, don't you think?

If you must have a vizier, fire FEGO and hire Truth. Truth is strong enough to overcome regret.

Clean or Change Your Lenses

If you wear contact lenses, you know how hard it is to see anything if your lenses are covered with protein deposits. If the lenses are old and torn, it is uncomfortable, even painful, to wear them. In the same way, scratched up eyeglasses are useless, too.

Without fear and ego to blind us, we can finally see clearly. When we clean the lens through which we view life, and when we put on the undamaged glasses of reality, the same old circumstances look remarkably different. We cannot change the past or the present, but we can perceive it more accurately and reinterpret our experiences. And we can draw better conclusions about how to be and do things differently in the future.

The truth is often not pretty. When we face up to our own contributions to our relationship messes, it can be a real challenge. Like most challenges, it offers an opportunity to rise above or bow down. If we bow down to a challenge, we abdicate power and decision-making authority with regards to moving forward in life, but we are free to choose whether to kneel to the challenge or to overcome it. Regret impedes; it freezes us up, so that we cannot move at all. Regret makes us like jellyfish, carried back and forth by the currents of circumstances.

The practice of unforgiveness, or holding onto regret, elevates your hurt inner child (or hurt outer adult) to a position of an emotional tyrant, which is responsible for making all of your decisions on sustaining/maintaining hurtful, unresolved relationship baggage. We hold onto unforgiveness, expressing regret for not getting the offender back, but unbridled lust for fairness, justice and personal vengeance hinders one from getting to the space of forgiveness. The desire for vengeance or payback is a limiting belief that impedes a true dismount. It impedes one's ability to surrender and let go. Surrender simply means that you are not in control. As legendary producer, composer, writer and musician Quincy Jones once told me,

> *God is the controller of everything. But if you ask for all of the control, God will give it to you and then you'll see how overwhelmed you are sitting in God's seat of controlling everything. What you don't want to happen is for the pilot, God, to leave the cockpit while you're sitting there navigating this plane (your life). God has a way of teaching you by giving you what you think you want so you can learn by trial and error, to know that the person, place or thing obtained isn't what you really want. "Man, I've seen God leave the room on a bunch of people, and then they became overwhelmed because it was too much for them to deal with. You better keep God as your pilot so you can ensure*

yourself a safe landing to whatever your destination may be.

Don't Just Do Something! Sit There!

Surrender sounds so passive, but it is not. Surrender silences all the surface noise, so that you can get the deep work done. Do you want to make the most of your time? Be still enough to uproot your regrets.

Time is the most valuable currency we have on planet Earth. Once you lose it, you can't get it back. I'd rather lose a million dollar than lose five years of meaningful/purposeful living. You can earn back lost money, but you cannot earn back lost time. And all the time you spend regretting, resisting, holding on to limiting beliefs, and letting FEGO lead you around by the nose is irretrievably lost time.

As long as you are working on the healing, whatever time it takes for you to heal, understand, forgive and grow is time well spent. But if all you are doing is letting time slip by, without doing the personal work, then you are merely spending your time frivolously and impeding your own growth. Commit yourself to brooding like a hen on her eggs until the answers and insights hatch. When you are objective and willing to be accountable, you may find something that helps you become a better person and which gives meaning and purpose to the painful experience you endured.

EXERCISE 7: PUTTING THESE IDEAS INTO PRACTICE

As you think about the ideas in this chapter, do you see FEGO lurking behind the scenes in your life? Please consider the following questions:

What past experience or trauma are you determined (maybe even desperate) to keep from happening again in the future?

_____

How does that fear affect the way you perceive or interpret what other people say and do?

_____

In what areas of your life do you feel tempted to distract yourself with surface noise and surface change?

_____

If you could not see very well, and there was an affordable treatment available that would make your vision better than ever before, would you undergo that treatment? Why or why not?

_____

How does your response to Question 4 above relate to your level of willingness to invest yourself in the process of shedding regret to restore clarity to your perception of yourself and others so that you can build better future relationships?

_____

_____

Chapter 8

Moving Forward Unhindered by Unresolved Issues and "Baggage"

> *...my ultimate and biggest regret is that I couldn't change the circumstances or situations surrounding my mother's death and I couldn't provide her with the type of life that I felt she deserved.*

When You Move Forward, Travel Light

Don't just check your baggage. Empty the bags, and be intentional about what you keep in your carry-on. Keep the golden nuggets that have helped you grow and will help you keep growing in the future. Keep the memories that help you maintain an attitude of gratitude. If you can be thankful for the memories of past good times, keep them; if a memory fills you with anger, resentment or hopelessness, let it fade.

Many people think that letting go is disconnecting. Letting go, disconnecting and avoidance are three different things. The body is a perfect metaphor for a healthy kind of release. The body takes in all that it needs, all that is good for it, and then filters out, to the best of its ability, all that is bad and passes it out as waste. The passing of what is left over after processing is release.

Some people interfere with the process. The body can take in something that might not be good for it, but it will still extract whatever nutrients it can get out of it. Bad relationships work the same way, on a spiritual level. Even in a bad relationship there are still spiritual nutrients that can be extracted, followed by a release of the negative aspects and relationship toxins. This reminds me of the words from world renowned revolutionary martial artist Bruce Lee *"Adapt what is useful, reject what is useless and add what is specifically your own."* Since avoidance interferes with the process of getting those nutrients, it may prolong that process or even hinder your ability to understand that a process is, indeed, in effect. So don't avoid difficult issues. As we have discussed elsewhere in this book, trauma, pain, hurt and suffering are, as the Buddha observed, stair steps to get to a higher level of understanding of life. Suffering, pain, disappointment, and betrayal all have a spiritual value that we must embrace, without avoidance, before releasing them after processing out (absorbing) their spiritual nutritional value.

Remember to Leave Space for Grieving

You may be thinking, *"All that lofty spiritual stuff is well and good, Zo, but this feels awful."* It is hard to be high-minded when you are caught up in painful emotions. As we discussed earlier in this book, a break up involves a grieving process. Even self-examination and transformation involves a kind of grief process. Break ups mean the death of the "we" that used to be, or at least, the death of one's idea of the "we" that used to be. Even if the relationship is transformed into something better, there is still the death of old, familiar patterns. If the relationship ends completely, there is the death of the dreams of what might be or of what might have been. An old poem put it this way, *"Of all sad words of tongue or pen, the saddest are these: It might have been[xxiii]."*

Unresolved Issues

There is an element of tension inherent in the word "unresolved." Like the missing last chord of a song, whatever is not resolved can leave you with the feeling that you are just hanging there, not securely planted and without a solid landing. It is an unsettling feeling, and resolution may not be entirely within your control.

Some key questions are:

What issues are unresolved?

For each unresolved issue, why is it unresolved?
Are you the one refusing to resolve it?
Are you willing to resolve it, and is the other person refusing to resolve it?

Is it something you are able resolve on your own (even if the other person chooses not to help you resolve it)?

If you can't resolve it alone, is the relationship issue so bad that the status quo is unacceptable?

If you let it ride, can you keep from letting frustration or disappointment eat away at you and poison this or other relationships?

Finding Peace in Doing All You Can

You can't make someone else change. You can't even make someone else want to change. But you can make sure you have made every effort to do everything you can to examine yourself and change the things in yourself that you think need changing, including your attitude and perspective. It is amazing how the very same set of circumstances can look very different when you look at them through a different set of lenses. It is not so much that anything has changed, it is just that a transformed perspective lets you see and interpret persons, places, things and ideas differently, so that you can respond to them differently without the resentment or the initial resistance.

Some Christian believers might say, *"You have to get along, because God says we're supposed to live at peace with everybody."* If they are referring to the Bible verse in Romans 12:18, they are almost right. What that passage actually says is, *"If it is possible, as far as it depends on you, live at peace with everyone*[xxiv].*"* Even if you decide that the circumstances have to change, there is great peace in knowing that you have done all you can. That knowledge can help free you from guilt and regret.

Acceptance

We talked earlier about acceptance being the final stage of grief. We also mentioned the Serenity Prayer, which not only calls us to seek the courage to change what we can but also to seek the serenity to accept the things we cannot change (and the wisdom to know the difference).

Acceptance says, without bitterness or resentment, *"I wish it could have been different, but I accept that it is what it is, and that it won't be different, no matter what I do. Wishing won't make it so."* There might be wistfulness, or sadness, or disappointment, but no regrets.

The Regret Bucket List

At the end of this chapter, I will offer an opportunity to identify your regrets, with the intention of walking you through them. When I say "walking you through them," I do not mean, "blowing past them." I mean taking slow, deliberate, measured steps, being hospitable to the pain associated with each thought and memory that brings regret, as if the pain were an honored guest in your home. No one says you have to like having that person stay with you, but nevertheless, while the guest is there, you feed and care for your guest, trying to understand them objectively and respond to the needs your guest presents. Similarly, you are not there to judge yourself or your regret, but simply to take the time to embrace it, and watch it unfold to reveal the gift of insight and understanding you need to move forward.

I call the list of regrets like these the Regret Bucket List, and its purpose is to enable you to live life to the fullest through self-awareness and self-forgiveness. Laying down regret means self-acceptance. It requires surrender. Unconditional forgiveness is like unconditional love. There are no stipulations. You can only give it fully, or you can't give it at all.

A lot of people have heard about the concept of the "bucket list." If not, see the movie by the same name starring Morgan Freeman and Jack Nicolson. It's one of my favorite movies. The "bucket list" means creating a list of things that you've always wanted to do and then one by one, checking them off as a symbol that you have lived a full, complete and amazing life. Well, I don't believe you can live a full, complete or amazing life if you have a life filled with regrets. It is difficult to say that you've lived a fulfilled life if you've held on to a lot of personal baggage, if you resent/resist a lot the lessons in your relationship curriculum, carrying this unfinished work with you on your journey, regardless if you've had the ability to travel all over the world and experience everything on your conventional bucket list it, your life may still be considered unfulfilled without checking off all of the items on your regret bucket list.

When I was a young buck in the 1980s I remember a now classic song by The Romantics called "What I Like About You."[xxv] Conversely, the purpose of the Regret Bucket List is to remove from your internal self-talk playlist the classic anthem of "What I

Don't Like About Me." It's a journal of your regrets but categorized like a basic bucket list with the goal of checking off all of your regrets through the pathway of self-awareness, self-acceptance and self-forgiveness.

Looking at regrets in an objective way can bring healing as you take responsibility for co-creating the situation by virtue of taking part of it, experiencing it, interpreting it, and reacting to it. In light of the resulting insights and self-awareness, it is possible to re-contextualize your relationship experiences and begin to move forward in a healthier, more enlightened way. People who look back subjectively tend to cement their relationship experiences into a pattern of belief that says, *"I was right, and I was wronged."* Opportunities for growth, change, and healing are stunted when we refuse to move beyond a stubborn insistence that our own point of view is correct and the failure of the relationship is the other person's fault. Looking back objectively provides a different perspective that reveals how I could have behaved or responded differently to change the outcome or, at least, to understand it better.

The only way you can check a regret off this bucket list is through self-forgiveness. Submission, self-acceptance, humility, and objectivity are all things that are connected to self-forgiveness. You can't forgive others until you forgive/accept yourself fully. And any mistake that was made in a relationship by you or someone else can always be re-contextualized and looked at from a different perspective that could actually help you evolve. Ignoring the pain or distracting ourselves from the pain robs us of a real gift: the opportunity to become "universatile," a word I use to mean universal in perspective and versatile in the application of that perspective.

Self-awareness and self-forgiveness lets you live life from a state where you understand that what happens to you also happens because of you. It doesn't just happen to you like: *"Well, this happened to me and I had nothing to do with it."* Being able to check off all of the things that you are responsible for gives you tremendous power and freedom and gives you an ability to grow from situation to situation. Remember: Regret is a holding pattern. And what are you holding? You're holding onto pain as well as elevating pain to a position of power and authority in your life. Let it go to set yourself free.

Checking Regrets Off of the Bucket List

As was mentioned earlier, when you're writing about your regrets, the only way to check these regrets off your bucket list is through self-forgiveness. Relationship trauma is yin to the yang of forgiveness. And we cannot forgive unless we get to a space where we've accepted relationship trauma as a necessary developmental tool for our lives.

I can't stress this point enough: You can't forgive anybody until you first forgive yourself. You simply can't completely embrace anyone's soul until you've embraced who you really are at your core; at the bottom of yourself. You can't completely love, you can't fully share, you can't totally emphasize and ultimately you can only give so much. Furthermore, you can only reach a certain level of intimacy.

To borrow Krishnamurti's phrase, *"truth is a pathless land"*[xxvi] with regards to who you are. This book can't tell you the truth of who you are but this Regret Bucket List can, if you're open, honest, and authentic when you're writing out what it is that you regret. Completeness will only beget itself, but brokenness will only beget brokenness. As I said in my first book, *The Rebirth of Seeds*, two broken people can't come together and form a whole person.[xxvii] We're going to continue to cut each other on the shards of the surface of our shadow selves until we reconcile the shadow with the dawning light from within.

My Personal Regrets

One of my greatest regrets is that most of my long-term relationships have ended argumentatively, in very negative ways. I regret the way break ups like that usually result in losing all of the connections that I've made with the other person's family, as well as losing the relationship I had with the other person.

Another one of my greatest regrets that I've been working to check off my list is my tendency to push my oldest son. I push him hard because I don't want him to hit pitfalls that I hit when I was his age. And sometimes I want him to reach certain benchmarks that I missed when I was his age. I regret pushing him a little too hard, so I have to come to terms with that and understand that he's still a kid and he should be able to enjoy being a kid. I have to stop trying to live vicariously through him.

But my ultimate and biggest regret is that I couldn't change the circumstances or situations surrounding my mother's death and I couldn't provide her with the type of life that I felt she deserved. The only solace that I was able to receive from her death is that, because she was so sick and so ill, I was grateful when death ended her pain.

Even though my mother made some life choices that put her in traumatic situations and ensnared her in abject poverty, she managed to get us all out of the projects, without any of her children being on drugs or in prison. I felt indebted to her for lifting everybody up without help from the three men who fathered her six children. When she died, I felt like I let her down because I wasn't able to provide her with a more comfortable environment in her later years, and that limiting belief spills over into my other relationships. My last relationship ended because I was thinking: *"I've got to create a perfect environment in order for the relationship to move forward,"* when the sister simply wanted to be with me in whatever environment it was. My limiting belief prevented her from loving me the way she wanted to love, to the point that she got tired of wanting to love me.

EXERCISE 8: MY REGRET BUCKET LIST

As I work through my own Regret Bucket List, I use a journaling format that looks something like this:

□   1. I regret that I have not been living my life for myself but have been trying to please everyone else.

_____

_____

COMMENTS

_____

_____

_____

In Progress □   *Checked Off* □

□   2. Being too afraid to experience any type of new adventures is one of the biggest regrets I have in my life.

_____

_____

COMMENTS

_____

_____

_____

In Progress □   *Checked Off* □

□   3. Depending on someone else to make my life happy instead of just choosing to BE happy has proven not to be a good thing.

_____

_____

COMMENTS

_____

_____

_____

In Progress □   *Checked Off* □

□   4. In the past, I built such an impenetrable wall around my heart that I kept everything out—not just the hurt.

_____

_____

COMMENTS

_____

_____

_____

In Progress □   *Checked Off* □

☐   5. I have allowed distractions from my past or fascinations with the future to prevent me from enjoying the gift of my present.

_____

_____

COMMENTS

_____

_____

_____

In Progress ☐   *Checked Off* ☐

EXERCISE 9: CREATING YOUR BUCKET LIST

What are your regrets? What are you willing to face right now? Write it down and live your life to check off each one of these regrets through self-forgiveness. That's the only way you're going to live a truly fulfilling life. And when you're able to forgive yourself for all of the things on your list, imagine the levels of love that you're going to be able to experience and then resonate out into the world. I always tell people, *"You get what you are. You magnetize who you are."* And if you are a bucket list full of regret, guess what you're magnetizing back into your experience? If you are living this type of life, you have imprisoned yourself. You are surrounded by bars made of poisonous, limiting beliefs that will continue to mold and shape the experience and the existence that you are currently living. The only way out is to take the key that is in your pocket and unlock the door. That key is self-forgiveness, which can lead to unconditional forgiveness of others, which may ultimately lead to unconditional love itself. If you want this life for yourself, I simply offer you the knowledge of this key's existence within yourself now:

Name five things that you really dislike about yourself.

1. _____

2. _____

3. _____

4. _____

5. _____

Name two of your main character flaws.

1. _____

2. _____

Most of us dislike ourselves most of the time, but refuse to take responsibility for the tragedy that manifests itself in our relationship because we are so heavily invested in the idea of who we would like to be. We focus so much on the self we would like to be, that we cannot see or try to hide from who we really are. To keep up the masquerade, we try to blame others when we get something less than the ideal. But all we accomplish by such activity is to draw to ourselves more of what we really are, the part of us we are refusing to look in the face.

Through the Regret Bucket List, you can stop hiding or playing games and take an objective look by listing five personal flaws or character challenges that could fit in the category of what Carl Jung called "The Shadow." This is where you can list those hurts, pains and regrets that cause you feelings of guilt or shame and sit down and reconcile with those regrets and feelings. If, and when, you can weather the storm of getting to that state, it's going to be beautiful once you've arrived. It's going to be awesome!

EXERCISE 10: PUTTING THESE IDEAS INTO PRACTICE

Using a journal format like the one I used, or using the questions below, create and start working through your own Regret Bucket List. As you list five regrets or character flaws that are operating as limiting beliefs in your life, consider how these thoughts affect/warp the way you see and interpret the world around you and the people in your life. Then, move toward self-awareness, self-forgiveness and release, using the following steps:

1. **First regret on my Regret Bucket List**

   I used to think:
   [List regret.]

   _____

   I now see that my contribution to the situation was:
   [Describe what you brought to the
   problem]_____

   _____

   This awareness has helped me learn:
   [Describe what you learned and the new insights you have
   gained.] _____

   _____

   I hereby commit on _____[date] to lay this regret aside
   and replace it with forgiveness for my contribution to the
   situation and gratitude for the growth this awareness has
   brought into my life.

   In the future, I will think and respond differently in the
   following ways: [List intended new ways of thinking,
   speaking, and behaving.]

_____

_____

2. **Second regret on my Regret Bucket List**

I used to think:
[List regret.]

_____

I now see that my contribution to the situation was:
[Describe what you brought to the
problem]_____

_____

This awareness has helped me learn:
[Describe what you learned and the new insights you have
gained.] _____

_____

I hereby commit on _____[date] to lay this regret aside
and replace it with forgiveness for my contribution to the
situation and gratitude for the growth this awareness has
brought into my life.

In the future, I will think and respond differently in the
following ways: [List intended new ways of thinking,
speaking, and behaving.]

_____

_____

3. **Third regret on my Regret Bucket List**

I used to think:

[List regret.]

_____

I now see that my contribution to the situation was:
[Describe what you brought to the
problem]_____

_____

This awareness has helped me learn:
[Describe what you learned and the new insights you have
gained.] _____

_____

I hereby commit on _____[date] to lay this regret aside
and replace it with forgiveness for my contribution to the
situation and gratitude for the growth this awareness has
brought into my life.

In the future, I will think and respond differently in the
following ways: [List intended new ways of thinking,
speaking, and behaving.]

_____

_____

4. **Fourth regret on my Regret Bucket List**

I used to think:
[List regret.]

_____

I now see that my contribution to the situation was:
[Describe what you brought to the
problem]_____

This awareness has helped me learn:
[Describe what you learned and the new insights you have gained.] _____

I hereby commit on _____[date] to lay this regret aside and replace it with forgiveness for my contribution to the situation and gratitude for the growth this awareness has brought into my life.

In the future, I will think and respond differently in the following ways: [List intended new ways of thinking, speaking, and behaving.]

5. **Fifth regret on my Regret Bucket List**

I used to think:
[List regret.]

I now see that my contribution to the situation was:
[Describe what you brought to the problem]_____

This awareness has helped me learn:
[Describe what you learned and the new insights you have gained.] _____

I hereby commit on _____[date] to lay this regret aside
and replace it with forgiveness for my contribution to the
situation and gratitude for the growth this awareness has
brought into my life.

In the future, I will think and respond differently in the
following ways: [List intended new ways of thinking,
speaking, and behaving.]

_____

_____

Chapter 9

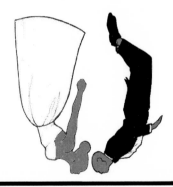

Moving Forward | Alone or Together
(Do I need to give this relationship the boot or a reboot?)

> *It's not your partner's job to grow with you, or to change when you change.*

A Musical Tour of the Question: To Break Up or Not to Break Up?

If we can believe that love songs are the heart's cry, then the answer to this question is all over the map. Singers like the incomparable Sade urge lovers to persevere; to "hang on to your love,"[xxviii] and to consider the sad consequences of a break up. Casting manly pride aside, even old-school crooners like the Temptations declared that they *"Ain't too proud to beg"*[xxix] for the relationship to continue.

Nonetheless, eroded expectations and disappointments can take their toll on love and hope in a relationship, as the precocious Michael Jackson expressed when he and his brothers sang, "Never can say goodbye."[xxx]

The point of this brief journey through love song/break up song history is that the crisis point in a relationship is a significant crossroad, where things can go either way. There can be good reasons to stay together. There can be bad reasons to end a relationship. There can be bad reasons to stay together, and there can be good (or at least wise and justifiable) reasons to break up, even when it is, as Neil Sedaka pointed out, "hard to do."

One of the important by-products of the self-reflection time in the cocoon is to reach a point of clarity so that one is able to distinguish the good reasons from the bad reasons, and to make a decision that seeks to put both people in the relationship in the best position to grow and flourish, whether moving forward happens together or apart.

What Is Your Level of Investment in and Commitment to This Relationship?

Before you answer that question, make sure that reasoned analysis precedes reckless abandon. Intuition may play a huge role in this analysis, and I don't mean to say otherwise, however, I am just cautioning all my brothers and sisters (and reminding myself) that we all stand in peril of thinking with the wrong body parts sometimes. Clear thinking produces better decisions that will still seem like good decisions when the rosy haze of emotion, bravado, or lust have faded. Saying "I'm all in" may sound good in the heat of the moment, but rebuilding a relationship can be a long and difficult process. Try not to let your words commit you to more than you are willing to back up with your actions.

Remember the art of *Kinsukeroi* that we mentioned when we were talking about forgiveness? It is the costly process of mending broken ceramic vessels with precious metals. One thing to consider when trying to evaluate your future commitment to this relationship is whether you have already invested a great deal of the "precious metal" of your heart, soul, and life in this relationship, or whether you are willing to make that kind of investment in the future. If you believe that this relationship is worth that level of investment and commitment, then a relationship reboot may be a better choice than giving the relationship the boot.

But there are more factors to consider before reaching a final decision.

Are You in Danger?

No matter what cultural norms and statistics may say to the contrary, physical and emotional violence are unacceptable. It is not okay to live in a relationship fearful for your own life, physical safety or for the life and physical safety of your children, or other loved ones. The patterns and dynamics of violence and abuse make objective decision-making very difficult, and it is beyond the scope of this book to explore this very important topic in great detail. But it is too important not to say:

> If you have been the victim of physical violence or emotional abuse in this, or another relationship, seek professional help.

> If you are the perpetrator of physical violence or emotional abuse in this, or another relationship, please seek help.

Some miraculous transformations occur, but they are probably not the norm. Many people never change or even acknowledge engaging in abuse or violence. Many people never overcome the experience of violence or abuse to allow the restoration of trust or forgiveness to occur.

Even if you decide that your level of commitment to the other person is high enough to keep your heart open to seek restoration of a relationship when threats of physical harm have passed (which may take a long time, depending on the progression, or lack thereof, of each individual's journey toward true healing and transformation), remember that **physical safety is paramount**. How can people reconcile and restore a relationship if one is dead or in a coma because of physical violence?

What about "Emotional Abuse"?

In this question, I put the phrase "emotional abuse" in quotes because the analysis may vary, depending on what one means by "emotional abuse." In any relationship, people are likely to feel hurt, even abused or rejected when their partner goes through a season of selfishness or thoughtlessness. That kind of hurt is a real thing that needs to be dealt with, if the relationship is going to grow and move forward to a place of mutual respect, joy and fulfillment. But if both people are willing to open their eyes, look at what they are doing, and the impact it has on the other person, and, if whoever is acting selfishly or thoughtlessly is willing to look at those reflections that are coming back to him or her and strive toward growth and change, then this may be less a matter of actual emotional abuse, and more a matter of bearing with someone who is growing at a different pace.

You can only work on yourself and control what is yours to control. Your progress is not contingent upon your partner's participation or lack thereof. It's not your partner's job to grow with you, or to change when you change. Your growth is not contingent upon anyone else's participation or choices.

Often people hold onto their partner thinking things like:

> If you work with me to change, our relationship will get better.

> I'll change when you change.

> If you show me you're committed, then I'll show you I'm committed.

No, at the end of the day, relationships are a classroom, and the curriculum is yours. If you want to become a better person in relationship, it is your responsibility to become a better person in life, and then you'll attract better people to relate to because what you're attracting reflects who you are right now. Dealing with those reflections is a type of curriculum that helps you evolve; this is how you move forward. The same is true of your partner, who is getting a reflection from you. Your, and your partner's, job is to take that highly reflective information and re-contextualize your idea of yourself by what you're receiving from your partner. And guess what? Your partner will do it at a different rate than you do. You do it at a different rate than your partner does. Your sister does it at a different rate than your mother. Your brother does it at a different rate than your father. You can't wait for someone else to evolve, grow and meet you somewhere, while you are still in flux yourself, processing your own lessons. It is normal for two people to be growing and changing at totally different rates.

The key, though, is whether you and your partner have developed a way of interacting that gives each of you the freedom to be about the work of growth and change. If one is intentionally acting to control, stifle or manipulate the other, then that is a clear warning flag that this is not a safe or healthy relationship, at least until the other person is truly willing to care about the impact of his or her behavior, and to consider the possible need to grow, change or do something differently. To put it in simpler terms, just because we go together doesn't mean we grow together.

If you are experiencing your partner's words or behavior as emotionally abusive, but your partner sincerely does not intend to hurt you, you have to ask yourself frankly, *"Can I live, grow and flourish in this relationship while I wait for my partner's eyes to be opened?"* Sometimes people just have such different ways of perceiving the world that the one causing the pain is blind to what the other person sees or experiences. Suppose one person perceives themselves as logical and rational, and only trusts or believes information gained through sensory observation, the scientific method or reason alone, while the other person perceives himself or herself as acutely emotionally discerning and intuitive. There may be great potential for miscommunication, hurt and frustration on both sides! It would be like a Star Trek relationship between Mr. Spock (the logical Vulcan) and Counselor Deanna Troi (the emotional empath). If either person decides to discount the other person's perceived experience, there is a train wreck ahead. To treat another person's experience or understanding as impossible or non-existent is to marginalize the other person and lead. To be sure, any of us can be deceived, misguided, or just plain wrong. But in a relationship based on love and respect, the way to deal with blind spots is with an attitude like, *"I care about what you are experiencing. But I can't yet see it the way you see it. Could you please try to help me understand what it looks and feels like to you and why it looks and feels that way?"* Too often, though, the response reflects an attitude of, *"I don't see it, and I think you are just making it up, so I'm not going to waste time on figments of your imagination."* Bottom line: The message transmitted is *"You do not matter enough to me to be worth my time and effort to grow beyond my accustomed ways of seeing and perceiving things."*

Watch out when those kind of stubborn attitudes begin to show up in your relationship environment. If you are the one with that attitude, uproot it from the inside out! It is toxic and will stunt your growth. And if it is your partner who has no interest in accepting the reflections that are coming back to them from the relationship, that is like a kid sitting in a classroom and saying, *"I'm not going to let you teach me. I'm not going to read these textbooks."* That is a strong warning flag that it may be time to dismount, unless you are willing and able to grow and change on your own, no matter what your partner says or does.

The clearest case of when it is time to break up in an emotionally abusive situation is when your partner wants to control you, intends to stifle or manipulate you, and is messing with your mind intentionally. Patrick Hamilton's play *Gas Light* (sometimes known as *Angel Street*), and the films presenting the same story, depict a husband's deliberate efforts to make his wife doubt her ability to perceive reality like a sane person,[xxxi] and the term "gaslighting" developed as a way to describe an extreme form of psychological abuse and control.

The "gaslighter" is not blind or clueless, but knows exactly what he or she is doing, and the intent is to do harm. As with a situation involving physical abuse, your safety is paramount. Seek help and take precautions that will keep you safe. If you decide to hang in there for the possibility of a relationship reboot, proceed with caution, looking for evidence of real change. At the same time, if, miraculously, there is real and lasting change, beware of any tendency to hold a grudge about past behavior. Without real change *and* real forgiveness, rebooting a relationship after deep hurt can be a recipe for stalling out in pain and resentment, or may involve the perpetuation of behaviors that should not be reinforced, enabled, or tolerated.

What about Plain Old Dissatisfaction, Restlessness, Boredom, Disappointment or...?

New relationships can be exciting. *Really,* exciting. Our bodies release all kinds of feel-good chemicals – happy ones, sexy ones, and contented ones... But it is not a non-stop rush and high. Sooner or later the high-flying honeymoon feelings slow down or end. Are you ready for a different feeling in the next phase of the relationship? Or are you accustomed, or even a little addicted to the "high," so that you are now restless, bored or dissatisfied and ready to move on to the next relational thrill?

These are the shallower reasons for breaking up. It can be a compelling enough reason if one or both partners can't move past the restlessness.

These lower levels of relationship can also work to entangle you and make you want to stay in a relationship when it is time for it to end. By "lower levels of relationship," I mean a surface kind of emotionality, sentimentality, or physicality that says things like:

"Aw, she's so beautiful."

"I don't know what I will do without him."

"That was the prettiest, the most beautiful girl I've ever been with."

"I'm never gonna find someone that's as sexy or as sensual as he is."

You can get locked into the lower vibratory levels of energy, where the attachment is pretty shallow and beast-like. If you ask a guy why this woman is important to him, and he says, *"Oh, she cooked, and she gave me sex,"* or *"She was so beautiful on my arm when we went out,"* it might make you wonder whether he is much more evolved than a barnyard animal (and maybe not quite as relationally developed as the average dog or cat).

I get it that we all need food to live, and most of us need – or at least, *want* sex. But if getting good food, good sex and having a prestigious trophy-object next to you when you go out is all you want out of a relationship, you may want to ask yourself whether you are really living up to your full human potential.

Conflict or restlessness in a relationship can lead you to discover deeper levels beyond this superficial kind of attraction. When you start looking at a person and how they elevate you through the relationship, then you will understand the purpose of conflict. It can provide a good kind of stress that can propel you to the next level. That is something to embrace, not something to run away from. Even in the medical studies of stress, they will tell you that certain levels of stress are actually good for you. When they tell the elderly to get out and take a brisk walk, that's because they want them to elevate their heart rate. When you elevate the heart rate, you stress the heart, but it can be a good kind of stress. In a similar way, certain levels of conflict or discord can actually benefit us.

Some important diagnostic questions may be:

Am I currently living up to my full potential?

Or am I just coasting along the path of least resistance?

Am I seeking lower-level pleasure and satisfaction because it is easier than wanting more out of a relationship and out of myself?

Good food and good sex are even more enjoyable when shared between partners who experience one another as treasured and respected *persons*, rather than as objects. Pleasure is a good thing! But you and your partner are more than mere instrumentalities to be used for satisfying whims and desires.

True Confessions: My World-Shifting Break up That Led to This Book

I want the reader to connect to me deeply and spiritually beyond just the words. I experienced a break up that was world altering, mind-altering, and shattering to my entire being. I don't want to mislead anyone who reads this book. I am not someone who has arrived at perfection. I am a man full of flaws, shortcomings, and of things that put me in direct need of the grace of God. That relationship and break up knocked me down a peg, spiritually, because of how I dealt with things. The heartbreak in my life from that break up sent me on such a soul-introspective reconnaissance mission that I realized that I don't have all the answers. I don't want to paint a picture full of articulate eloquence that will make the reader think that I have somehow overcome all of my inborn challenges. Rather, this book is an offering. It is an offering so that you may benefit, too, from my struggles. I hope that, by witnessing my journey, perhaps you may be helped in your own quest to figure out what your path is, which may very well be entirely different than my own. I also make it an offering for its own sake, so that I may heal as well, through the cathartic process of working through it and writing it down.

Part of the purpose of catharsis is purification and clarification. I had to reconnect and realign myself with who I was before, and who I have become after, the break up. When you have shared so much time, energy, passion, love, highs, lows, good, bad, ugly and indifferent...the whole gamut of life with another person, you become entwined, enmeshed and emotionally dependent with that person. You begin to identify with that person, and in some cases, you lose your own identity, because your identity became rooted in the relationship. So when such a self-defining relationship ends, you feel like you have ended in some way. It is like a piece of you is gone, and you wonder how to fill the void.

I learned to invest the energy in moving to the next level of understanding what this relationship – its birth, life, and death – had to teach me about who I was created to be and who I was becoming. It was not about filling the void with my old love, or with a new love, or with distractions and being busy for busyness sake. It was about receiving the break up as an inventory process.

Not every break up is forever. Sometimes a break up is like a reboot to a computer. Sometimes the break up is more like a time-out that lets you focus on your self-inventory without having to focus on the other person. But for it to be an unbiased self-inventory, you have to open your hand and your mind, and let go. Some break ups can be the foundation piece of a relationship reboot for you and your old love. It's not just about preparing for the conveyor belt of people who might want to be with you next. Don't foreclose the possibility of a restored, rebooted relationship (version 2.0) with your old love or the possibility of moving on separately to new and different relationship with other people. Seek to get to a place where you would be healthy and whole either way it turns out.

EXERCISE 11: PUTTING THESE IDEAS INTO PRACTICE

We have asked a lot of questions throughout this chapter, so this is just an opportunity to apply the questions directly to your own circumstances, experiences, and insights.

What are some good reasons I have for wanting to end (dismount) this relationship?

_____

_____

What are some good reasons I have for wanting to reboot this relationship?

_____

_____

What are some bad reasons I have for wanting to end (dismount) this relationship?

_____

_____

What are some bad reasons I have for wanting to re-boot this relationship?

_____

_____

Which is more likely to lead to the safety, health, growth, and fulfillment of both of us – a permanent break up or a relationship reboot? Why?

_____

_____

THE RELATIONSHIP DISMOUNT

Chapter 10

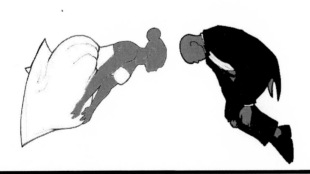

Break Ups That Make You Better, Not Bitter

Empowerment, by itself, can just as easily be used to enhance the power of someone who is in a toxic state of rage and bitterness...

How Will You Fly When You Emerge from the Cocoon?

If your time of self-reflection in the cocoon has led you to decide to break off your relationship, then you still have a very important question to consider. Will you emerge from the cocoon embittered or "embettered"? Will you be soaring into the future on the wings of freedom, grace and truth? Or will you be flying like a mad hornet on wings of anger, resentment, and vengeance? The way you approach the winding up of a relationship makes a profound difference – to you, to the other person in the relationship, and to all those who witness or are affected by the break up, and its aftermath.

Consider how far you have come during your time in the cocoon! If you are like most people, it is pain, hurt, suffering, major discomfort or dissatisfaction that has driven you to consider a break up . . . to consider picking up this book to go through the effort of self-reflection. In the midst of suffering, through the loss of a relationship, it is easy to lose perspective. You might call that being **embedded** in the problem.

When you react instead of reflecting and responding, it is common to feel as though you are in the middle of a battle. Whether your personal combat preference is to attack or to retreat, you are still dealing with the fight. At that point, you are **embattled**. A person who is very good at dominating (not to say that that is a praiseworthy thing) might stall out at being embattled, so long as he or she perceives himself or herself as "winning" the fight. Usually, it is when people get tired of the fight, whether they feel they are winning or losing, that people give up and withdraw emotionally from the relationship. But that withdrawal is rarely as tidy and dispassionate as it sounds, because the weariness, disappointment, hopelessness, or resentment that tends to fuel the withdrawal leads most people to become **embittered**. Sometimes people freely sling the noxious contents of their cups of bitterness all over the place. Sometimes people bury unresolved relationship hurt, disappointment and dissatisfaction deep inside, where it turns toxic, allowing bitterness to do its corrosive work of hollowing out their hearts and poisoning their minds. They may still look pretty good on the outside, but bumps in the road of life tend to jostle those hidden cups of bitterness, spilling the contents out during periods of life's turbulent times.

The truth is that you can run, but you cannot hide. The saying is trite but true: *"Wherever you go, there you are."* And right there with you is whatever baggage you have refused to set down, and whatever bitterness you have refused to transfuse out of the veins of your heart, mind, and emotions. *"In any given moment we have two options: to step forward into growth or to step back into safety."*[xxxii] Abraham Maslow.

Embedded | Embattled | Embittered

Is there more to your story and mine than bitterness, hopelessness, suffering, and despair? If you remember only one thing from this book, I hope it is this: that your hurts and struggles can be the keys to your growth, well-being, and "**embetterment.**" I want to distinguish "embetterment" as the goal, instead of merely seeking empowerment. Empowerment, by itself, can just as easily be used to enhance the power of someone who is in a toxic state of rage and bitterness, and it can be used to empower one who has actually grown in their understanding of grace and truth. A person who is seeking to become better is more likely to have goals that would be beneficial to bring to fruition through empowerment.

If you decide to leave a relationship, the ideal way to do so is to strive to raise yourself, and to the extent it is within your ability to bring it about, to elevate the other person. It might be a better place than before you met each other. Or it might only be better than you were when one or both of you realized it was time to close the relationship. But the point is to act thoughtfully, in every sense of that word, about how to end things.

Exhale, Excrete, and Empty Yourself

When we think about what is essential to life, we often think about things like food, water, shelter, and even air to breathe. When the basics are taken care of, then we start craving things we think will lead to meaning and fulfillment. But did you ever think about the vital role that emptiness plays in our lives? I do not mean emptiness as a constant state or as an end in itself, of course, but as a pre-condition to being filled. I cannot draw a full breath of fresh air until I exhale the previous breath that has spent itself. There is a limit to the food and water I can consume until it has passed all the way through me. As it passes I draw out all that is nutritious, life-giving, and beneficial, and then I excrete the leftover waste products. I cannot receive a wonderful gift if my hands are already full of other things. Emptiness, then, is a gateway to the next, and perhaps even more fulfilling fullness.

What is crucial is one's attitude and response to emptiness and endings. Death leads to decomposition, which can enrich the soil for future growth or contaminate the environment with toxins, depending on the nature of the dead material and how it is handled. The decomposition of a relationship is similar in many ways. Letting go of true love is a very long process. Sometimes it is a lifelong process. The key is never to regret.

You see, you will always remember a true love. Maybe you didn't have the different/oppositional/complementary tools to maintain the relationship. People have different tools based on how they were raised, their environment and life experiences. To say it simply, some people have the tools to resolve relationship conflict and some may not, but everyone has the potentiality to acquire the tools that they need. To add even more context to this thought, I think, some people are born with a working knowledge of the tools they need to navigate intimate relationships, while others have yet to discover them from within. Everyone has some tools, and everyone acquires and learns how to use those tools to the best of their ability, at different times and at different rates throughout life. Sometimes the experiences just don't link up right or synch up right, but it doesn't mean that the experience and the love itself was inauthentic, or a waste of your time. The love may have been real, but it's hard to maintain love without knowing what it is you need to work on, especially when it comes to how you contribute and participate within the relationship environment. Sometimes the break up is the catalyst for highlighting what it is you need to work on.

Even though you may never forget a true love that holds onto a piece of your heart all your life, it is not good to hold on to any regret. Regret can lead to resentment and resistance, creating a blockage when you hold onto them, instead of letting them pass through. Pardon the graphic metaphor, but it is as potentially harmful as not being able to have a bowel movement for a really long time.

Acceptance is another kind of releasing, emptying or exhaling. We may want answers or explanations to help us make sense of the pain or sadness, but sometimes we have to learn to accept that there may never be any definitive answer. Why did this happen to me? Why did this happen at all? What was the purpose of it? How did I come to deserve this type of experience? Sometimes you reach a level of understanding sooner or later, and other times you just stop having the desperate desire for an explanation.

I am drawn to many ideas presented in Eastern philosophies and religions, which have much to say in response to the suffering people experience in life. One such approach is to see good and bad, blessing and suffering, as essential components of the whole of life. To focus on or emphasize the importance or desirability of one over the other is to distort the total context in which both exist. Since we are part of all that is, it is really hard to get a sense of the totality of which we are a part, and to interpret it properly. I am in no way suggesting that I have all the answers or that I have the mystery solved. I am only saying that people may be prone to self-deception when they do not consider the possibility that what they think is bedrock reality, or ultimate truth, could turn out to be an illusion, or at least, a distortion.

One place where I think a dangerous distortion can happen is when one becomes too self-absorbed or self-focused in the face of suffering. The Sanskrit word for I/self, pride and ego is "*aham.*" To one familiar with American colloquial expressions, there is an amusing irony here. When I am focused on self, I am just being "a ham," drawing attention to myself and making everything all about me.

There is also a Sanskrit phrase, *Aham Brahmasmi*, which is known as one of the *mahavadyas* or "great sayings," which asserts that "I am *Brahma*," with *Brahma* connoting growth or limitless expansion of the ultimate reality. The traditional Hindu concept of *Aham Brahmasmi* seeks a level of self-awareness that produces detachment, so, in effect, relationship struggles are eliminated by merging all consideration of individual selves into the one cosmic reality[xxxiii], or as Frankie Beverley of the legendary soul group Maze sang "We are one." [xxxiv]But I digress... The merger of selves into the ultimate cosmic reality (GOD/LOVE) may be a bridge too far for a discussion on the seemingly endless machinations of the social game rules regarding intimate relationships, though, so I simply want to note that it is a common response, when we experience relationship trauma or hurt, to empower the *"aham"* ego side over the expansion side of our nature. I believe expansion and growth are very different from superficial change or simply moving on from a situation. To me, forgiveness, healing and growth happen when there is a balance of the ego and one's ability to evolve in understanding.

Some "Embetterment" Goals to Aim For

While your goals must ultimately be goals that you adopt and embrace authentically for yourself, I offer the following suggestions for possible aspirations you may find worthy of consideration when you are facing a decision to end a relationship:

> Leave the relationship truly wishing the other person well, with gratitude for lessons learned and any good times shared.

> Recognize your own past mistakes or unrealistic expectations, so you don't repeat them in the next relationship.

> Make sure the next relationship is a new, better relationship (instead of replaying negative, unfulfilling and/or disappointing relationship experiences multiple times with multiple people).

Things to Consider When You Are the One Initiating the Break up

If you are going to tell your partner the news that you are breaking up, be as kind, gentle and patient as possible. Maybe the other person could see it coming, but it is also possible that the idea of breaking up will be a shock. It is not a shock to you, of course, because you have been thinking about it for a while, and have probably had time to process the idea of breaking up, to start working through any grief or regret, and to get used to the idea of parting ways.

Because your partner will probably not be as far along in accepting the break up as you are, it is a kind and caring thing to be sensitive about when and how you mention your decision to break up. Think through what to say, and plan how to respond to things your partner might say or do, so that you won't react thoughtlessly or unwisely.

Things to Consider When the Other Person Initiates the Break up

If your partner wants to break up, then you are the one who may be in a position of shock, bewilderment, or hurt when you hear the news. Hopefully, your partner was as kind, gentle and sensitive as possible in telling you, but it probably feels terrible, just the same. A break up is the death of a relationship or that relationship's last exhale, and you will most likely experience the stages of grief as mentioned in an earlier chapter. Denial, bargaining, and anger are common responses, but your partner may not be open to negotiating or re-negotiating about preserving the relationship if he or she has firmly resolved to break up.

This is not to say that you should not explore the possibility of a relationship reboot now or in the future. Just be prepared that your partner may have already taken his or her emotional "stock" out of the relationship, and so may not be as eager or hopeful as you may be about your potential future together.

Things to Consider When the Break up is a Mutual Decision

When you both believe that it is time to break up, there may be mutual grief, weariness, relief, anger or frustration . . . any number of shared emotions. Depending on the dynamics of the relationship, you may find some comfort and closure in grieving together the loss of the relationship. If the shared emotions are more volatile and not conducive to bringing closure or healing, still make the effort to be as gracious and gentle as possible, trying to treat one another as you would want to be treated.

Am I Ready to Try Another Relationship?

So many people will ask me: "Well, when should I get back into a relationship?" I don't really know a certified answer. I would surmise that it's a person-by-person, couple-by-couple, and case-by-case situation. The deeper the relationship, the longer it went on, the more time you need to download, release, and take inventory. You might need a significant amount of time by yourself, getting comfortable with being alone, before you mount up again. A hurtful break up is an injury. It's an injury to your soul. In professional sports, many teams will not let an injured player get back on the court until the athlete can demonstrate certain acts of physical mobility. Questions one might ask an injured basketball player include: Can you run? Can you stop? Can you move laterally? Can you jump? If the basketball player cannot demonstrate an ability to do these things, without pain or physical limitations, that player has to sit down.

The same general idea applies to relationships. If you walk into a new relationship, still thinking about your old lover and wondering whether ending the relationship was the right thing to do, or questioning whether you made the decision of ending/starting a relationship to make someone else happy, then you're not ready for a new relationship.

If you're thinking any of the following things, you're not ready for a new relationship:

"Well, it's his or her loss."

"I was the victim."

"I have no personal accountability in the way things unraveled. It was all on him/her."

As long as there is inside you unforgiveness, resentment, fear, or a desire for revenge, any subsequent relationship is just a rebound. Work it through, and let it go. If your ex has a long term lease on a loft in your head space, you're not ready for a new relationship. If every conversation you have with your friends and family about relationships results in your bringing up your ex-partner, you're not ready for a new situation. If a chance meeting with your old lover stirs up thoughts of reconciliation, or stirs up unresolved issues, you are still carrying baggage that needs to be unloaded before you board the next love train.

If your lost love was a true love, it will always be part of you. But it does not need to control you or stop you from moving authentically into your future. Legendary singer (Whitney Houston's cousin) Dionne Warwick recorded a famous version of a song by Richard Kerr and Will Jennings called "I'll Never Love This Way Again." Some of the lyrics say:

> A fool will lose tomorrow
> Reaching back for yesterday
> I won't turn my head in sorrow
> If you should go away

I'll stand here and remember
Just how good it's been
And I know I'll never love this way again.[xxxv]

EXERCISE 12: PUTTING THESE IDEAS INTO PRACTICE

Think about a break up you have experienced in the past or one that you may be facing now, and consider the following questions:

Did you stall out/get stuck in one of the earlier phases we mentioned (embedded, embattled, or embittered)? If so, which one?

_____

_____

_____

What would it have taken in your former relationship, or what will it take in the break up you may be facing, to move all the way through to "Embitterment"? What were/are your points of greatest struggle?   How   can   you   overcome   them?

_____

_____

List at least three things (such as lessons learned or good times shared) from the relationship that broke up for which you are grateful.

_____

_____

_____

_____

When you have reached a point of forgiveness and release, consider writing a letter of forgiveness and blessing, in which you wish your former partner well. (You may decide that it is wise not to share this letter with your former partner, or with anyone else, but the main point of writing it is your own healing and closure.)

If you are facing a break up now, plan what you will say and do when you interact with your partner. What do you want to say? How do you want to come across? What do you want to avoid saying or doing? What might your partner say and do during the break up process? How would you respond to the words or actions you might anticipate? How can you demonstrate kindness, gentleness, sensitivity, and wisdom during the break up process?

BREAK UPS THAT MAKE YOU BETTER, NOT BITTER

Chapter 11

Rebooting the Relationship from a Transformed Perspective

> *Seek alignment over egotistical self-righteousness.*

What Makes a Reboot Work?

Have you ever had your computer or smartphone stop working or get bogged down, running poorly and inefficiently until you shut it down completely and then restarted it? Most of the time, a reboot seems to fix the problem[xxxvi], as if by magic. How does that work? For one thing, it stops everything that was running before, at the time of the problem. It clears away the programs, routines, and other background noise that you couldn't see, but that were consuming too many of your system's resources. To that extent, rebooting a relationship is like rebooting a computer, giving you a fresh start with less clutter and distraction.

But there is a big difference between computers and people: the computer (so far as I know) does not feel bad about starting over and does not remember, resist or resent all the bumpy places where the code got hung up. It is just code. You start it, and if it was programmed well, it runs the way it should.

People are not unfeeling machines. They can feel shame or anger about past failures. They remember the spots where past relational "systems" got hung up, and that very recollection can create an anticipatory fear or expectation that may become a self-fulfilling prophecy. We expect the relationship to get stuck at a certain point, and behold – it does! So as life programmers, sometimes we program failure into the new relationship because we haven't reconciled/resolved the bugs in the old relationship operating systems that we've been using. In a way, we program the bugs into our relationship experience.

One reason we have spent so much time talking about reflecting and releasing, is to keep relationship baggage (bugs, i.e. outdated relationship software) from the past from hindering future relationships, including a future "rebooted" relationship with our lover. Most people in relationships that have reached a crisis point do not want a replay of the same old patterns; they want a relationship that is the best it can be, or at least, on its way to becoming the best it can be.

A too-quick reboot in a relationship may arise from sentimentality, loneliness or boredom, and that can lead to a quick reversion to old, unsatisfying ways of interacting.

Reboot . . . Not Just Re-Booty

In an episode of the television show "The Parkers," Nikki Parker reveals to her daughter Kim Parker that she had slept with her ex – her daughter's dad – the night before. Daughter Kim asks, *"Was it a booty call? Or was it a love connection?"* [xxxvii] This is an important question when one is resuming a relationship, because the two are very different things.

Rebooting a relationship should involve laying the foundation of love, respect, mutual understanding, and enhanced communication that makes love connections real and lasting on all levels – physical-sexual, mental, emotional, and spiritual. Without that foundation, jumping back into a relationship, and especially jumping back into sex, will trigger lots of good-feeling biochemical reactions [xxxviii]that can fool you into thinking that everything is fresh and wonderful, when nothing has really changed. And if nothing has changed, there is no reason to believe that the relationship won't fall back into its old patterns, sooner or later, just as the Nikki Parker character and her ex were parted again by the end of the television show episode.

Those biochemical reactions are powerful. Some neurochemicals associated with sex, like oxytocin and vasopressin, can contribute to cementing a bond between partners. You may have heard that "love is a drug." Well, in a sense, it is, or at least some of the chemicals like dopamine that flood our bodies when we are interested in someone, can act like drugs. The computer that is our brain can get re-wired, so we can't help but think, *"Gimme some more of that!"* And like anyone in the grip of an addiction, we are prone to make bad choices, as we become slaves to the craving.

A successful reboot takes getting "clean," so we don't keep hijacking the development of new patterns for healthier relationships. When sex is the culmination of a relationship that is built on a strong foundation, instead of substituting sex for a solid foundation for the relationship, the feel-good chemicals work the way they are supposed to, making an ecstatic bond that is well worth celebrating.

How to Accomplish the Reboot

The best approach is to wait until after you have emerged, clear-headed, from the cocoon to reboot the relationship. The goal of the time in the cocoon was to bring insight, perspective, and understanding. We have spent most of this book talking about that process in great detail, step by step. But the insights gained from self-reflection in the cocoon are only a roadmap for transformation. Seeing yourself and the relationship differently is essential, but it is only a starting point. Driving according to the new relational roadmap means developing new ways and habits of thinking, being, speaking, doing, and responding. It is the changed behavior that manifests a truly transformed self and a truly transformed relationship. But it is also important to have a transformed and enhanced understanding of the relational environment.

Dead Plants and Floating Fish

When you think about a perfect setting, you know the kind of environment you want. You have probably pictured it in your mind a thousand times – relaxing on your deck, surrounded by lush, beautiful plants. Or maybe you saw yourself mellowing out in the den with the glow of a mesmerizing aquarium filled with exotic tropical fish. So you bought the plants and the pots (or the tank and the fish) and brought them home. You got everything set up, and it was great . . . for a while. But after a while the plants wilted and withered. The fish died and floated in the scum.

Paradise was lost. What happened? Why did it happen?

You knew what you wanted it to be like, but you were not prepared to do what you needed to do to sustain and maintain it. Plants need care, and some of the care depends on the type of plant. Fish need care, and the specifics depend on the type of fish. You may have had the best of intentions, but unless you knew what to do, and did it properly and consistently, your plants and fish would be dead, in spite of your good intentions.

Relationships are pretty much the same.

So before you reboot that old relationship (or even before you seek out a new relationship, if that is the path you are taking), it is worth the time to understand a bit about the care and feeding of relationships. I will only be hitting the highlights and flagging what I see as the key issues. There are many good books and other resources that go much deeper into building skills in each of these areas. Going deep is the key to gaining understanding that will help you make real and lasting changes in the care and feeding of your relationships.

Four Pillars of a Healthy Relationship

As I see it, the foundation of a healthy relationship rests on four pillars:

- Respect

- Communication

- Accountability

- Forgiveness

If you are like most people, Aretha Franklin's song "Respect"[xxxix] is running through your head right now. Those lyrics remind us that the perception of respect may vary from person to person. I may emerge from the cocoon thinking, "I need to be more thoughtful and considerate of the other person's feelings." That is a good insight. But how do I actually do that? What does it look like? Especially, what does being thoughtful and considerate look like and feel like to the other person?

How do you find that out? The best way is to ask. Now I know that some relationships get into a dynamic where one person thinks, *"If the other person really loved me, he or she would know what I want and need, and I shouldn't have to spell it out."* But that really isn't fair to either person. What if I really want to do better, but I keep guessing wrong about your needs and desires. We are both frustrated.

But if I say, *"I think I have really let you down in showing that I care about you by being thoughtful and considerate. But I think I will keep letting you down if I use my definition of 'being thoughtful and considerate' to guide my efforts to change. Would you please help me understand what things make you feel like I'm treating you with thoughtfulness and consideration? I really want to do that better."*

This approach can build a bridge to practicing better communication and to showing respect more effectively.

Respect also means playing fair and resisting the urge to play the games that destroy relationships. You may have experienced these games yourself, in one relationship or another. You might have been the perpetrator. You might have been the victim. The kind of destructive games that reveal a lack of respect for the other person are things like power games, mind games, manipulation, guilt trips, control tactics, using or abusing the other person, or letting the other person use or abuse you. The "gaslighting" we talked about in Chapter 9 is an example of a destructive manipulative game that shows serious lack of respect.

Respect is so important to healthy relationships that I think it should be considered the functional religion of relationships. How could a relationship ever falter if both partners were committed to a consistent practice of respecting each other's feelings, upbringing, emotional state, struggles, growth process, and personhood? If two people recognize the image of God in each other and respect that, it would transform and elevate the relationship. If respect were the religion of your relationship, taking responsibility would be relatively easy, because each partner would respect the other too much to pass the buck onto her or him in a clandestine way. If respect were the religion of your relationship, it would be easy to clarify your needs.

Mutual respect would enhance accountability, because we would not feel the need to dodge or deflect responsibility by using tactics like "tit for tat" or "kitchen sinking."

"Kitchen sinking" refers to responding to an issue presented by your partner with a whole bunch of gripes and complaints that you've held onto. It is often an indicator that you have not completely forgiven your partner for those things. But is it usually a tactic to deflect the discussion away from the topic presented by your partner, because you feel uncomfortable or attacked, or because you just don't want to address it. By bringing up everything including the kitchen sink (hence the name, "kitchen sinking"), communication shuts down before you get around to addressing what your partner presented to you. Kitchen sinking will destroy a relationship because it keeps you in this holding pattern regarding the issues that are presented.

"Tit for tat" is similar, but it is more often used as a technique for deflecting accountability. Instead of dealing with and taking responsibility for what's being presented to you, the natural inclination is to be defensive and bring up something that your partner is doing in the same capacity but maybe in a different situation. You could also call that argumentative counter-punching, with the expectation that the counter-punch will either draw attention away from one's own faults or that the two wrongs will cancel each other out somehow.

Consider the following example of the way tit for tat and kitchen sinking can play out in a conversation. Suppose I am trying to tell my girlfriend that I feel that she treats me inconsiderately when she gets so focused on her schoolwork that she seems to stop thinking about anything else, including me. If she responds, "Well, you get inconsiderate, too, when you're busy or preoccupied," then that would be more of an example of tit for tat. But if she says, *"Well, wait a minute. If I'm not considerate, what about the fact that you haven't introduced me to your mother. Don't you think that's inconsiderate? And when am I going to go to your job? You said you were going to take me to your job. I've never been there yet, and I'd like to go. Everyone else gets to go; how come I don't?"* There may even be other unresolved or hitherto unmentioned issues that may get thrown into the mix, seemingly without limit. The result of kitchen sinking is that there are so many issues bouncing around that it becomes overwhelming, so none of them get addressed. At that point, talking seems pointless, so you stop wanting to talk.

Stalling out in frustrated silence (tolerance of unresolved issues) invites what I call the volcano effect, because it is as if there is a silent clock ticking on a volcano that has lava and pressure building up inside its magma chamber. The pressure will continue to build until, one day, it's going to blow. That's what happens when our issues are not resolved in relationship. We feel like if we avoid them, don't talk about them, and if we isolate and insulate ourselves from the problem, the people and the conversation, everything will just blow over. Sometimes that may happen but more times than not, it doesn't happen that way. Commonly, the volcano effect will result in an explosion later on—an explosion of conflict, frustration, or lack of fulfillment. Sometimes we retreat to silence, thinking we are avoiding conflict or demonstrating tolerance. But I think acceptance is better than mere tolerance. In a state of acceptance, we can communicate without either person having to dominate the discussion or win the other person over to his or her point of view. Acceptance values the person and the relationship enough to be comfortable with having some unresolved differences, as long as they exist in an environment of mutual respect.

Mutual respect promotes honest communication and authentic sharing, unhindered by fear of being rejected or marginalized. Respectful communication often requires self-control, thoughtful planning, and agreed upon ground rules. A mutually agreed timeout can allow tempers to cool and gives each person the time and space to prepare for a constructive dialogue. But a timeout needs to be for a definite period of time; it is not an indefinite tabling of the issue to avoid dealing with it.

Maybe we depart from the issue, and we promise each other that we're going to pray on the issue, meditate on the issue, and research the issue if need be. And then we're going to come back fortified with information, new information outside of our own opinion, where we can come back and say, *"This is what I found. What do you think of this?"* or *"This is what I found. You read my notes; I'll read your notes."* And we come together as a collaborative where each person's opinion matters to the other person.

It matters what we say and how we say it. It is easier to talk to someone who's not constantly and inflexibly judging, criticizing and appraising everything you say as positive or negative; as right or wrong. If you look at everything that your partner is saying to you as an *offering*, as a gift, instead of a rigid demand disguised as an ultimatum, then the disrespect and judgment will be taken out of it. The walls come down, and you can start to hear each other and better understand each other's perspectives.

And if you present your own ideas clearly while using active, empathetic listening, to understand and show respect for your partner's views, you can then begin to move past suboptimal conflict responses like avoidance, acquiescence or domination and seek instead to find solutions that merge our partners concerns and interests with our own. Engaging in this way can ultimately give a relationship a deep and rich reservoir of trust and of respect, where the two people will accept being on the right path toward reaching a solution that both can agree on, even if they have not yet reached that destination of resolution on a particular issue.

Using Ground Rules to Create a Safe Space for Meaningful and Constructive Communication

You might consider setting some communication ground rules at the beginning of the reboot, before you actually need to use them.

- What room will be your "nonjudgmental communication room"?

- What behavior is expected in communication? No condemning talk or negative body language that shuts down communication. (You know – like I'm listening to you, but my arms are folded and I've got this look on my face that says, 'You're crazy.' None of that.)

- Take one issue at a time.

- The speaker's job is to help the listener understand the speaker's concerns, interests, preferences and perspective.

- The listener's job to try to stand in the speaker's shoes and understand the facts and feelings the speaker is sharing.

- Everybody gets a time limit. Maybe listening and feedback happen at different times. Maybe we switch roles in the same session, or maybe today's listener has to wait until the next scheduled time for a turn as speaker. By doing it in small increments, in a way that we have both agreed to do it, we may be able to process better and exercise more self-control. But if waiting is too hard, then maybe the ground rule needs to take that into account and allow more time for each increment and a turn for each partner in any given session.

Your ground rules need to be tailored to help you and your partner communicate effectively with each other and understand each other. But these are some ideas, as a starting point.

Accountability and Forgiveness – Before, During, and After the Reboot

We have already spent much of this book addressing the importance of accountability and forgiveness, but I want to emphasize a couple things to keep in mind as you reboot. Be on guard against any impediments to ongoing accountability and ongoing forgiveness.

If I have to be right (and I am quite a "rightaholic"), it can inhibit my willingness to take responsibility for my part of the problem. It is my belief that instead of being in pursuit of the right answer it's better to be in pursuit of being in alignment with your partner. Being in alignment has nothing to do with being right. You can be right and still be out of alignment with your partner. Seek alignment over egotistical self-righteousness. Fear of being punished or rejected can also make people less willing to be accountable or to admit any wrongdoing.

Emotional hijacking can happen when we feel attacked, threatened or fearful. It takes a little time, patience and self-control to resist making a knee-jerk reaction driven by the emotional centers in the old part of the brain where the limbic system is connected, to give time for the rational part of the brain, the frontal lobe, to engage and guide a measured response.[xl] If you have to outrun a menacing bear, an immediate, adrenaline-fueled flight response is a good thing that carries you out of harm's way. But a reflexive fight-or-flight response in a relationship is an impediment to open communication and the kind of accountability that leads to growth, change and forgiveness.

Let me be the first to admit that I have struggled with my temper. I have struggled with my sarcasm, condescension and arrogance. I have struggled with inflexibility in terms of my beliefs. I have struggled mightily and my relationships have suffered for it. I have to forgive myself for these past failings, and I have to be self-aware and accountable for future manifestations of these struggles.

Ideally, we would completely work through such struggles before a relationship reboot or before starting a new relationship. But sometimes growth comes incrementally, like peeling the layers of an onion. And sometimes we can only strive to win the battle with a particular struggle, without expecting the whole war to be won before we proceed – but then we must stay vigilant and ready to fight the next battle.

We must release past hurts. By carrying past hurts into future interactions, we may start (or continue) believing that the worst possible outcome will actually happen, and that mindset of anxiety and fear can so color our perceptions that we become paralyzed. Instead of choosing different perceptions and ways of responding that will lead us to growth, healing and freedom, we often bring about self-fulfilling prophecies by acting in ways that tend to produce the very outcome we fear and wish to avoid.

Staying Power

I realize now that, in order to have even the possibility of co-creating a relationship with staying power, I had to find the true purpose of who I am. I have to be able to live freely, openly and honestly in my relationship, and allow my partner to do the same. And then the ego will never be threatened or feel the need to have to defend itself. There is no need to manipulate one another into staying in a relationship or to pretend that a dead, hollow relationship is something it is not, for the sake of appearing to have a relationship with staying power. The ironic thing is that we are most likely to have staying power in a relationship when we open our hearts and hands, striving earnestly, but without grasping vainly. And whether that relationship stays or goes, it will do so, either way, in peace.

It is from this kind of position of freedom and strength that a relationship, and the individuals in it, can flourish and thrive.

EXERCISE 13: PUTTING THESE IDEAS INTO PRACTICE

While our focus here is the reboot of a relationship, the pillars of a healthy relationship are relevant to new relationships as well as rebooted ones. Take a minute to think about how the ideas in this chapter relate to your life and experiences.

What might lead you to want to reboot too soon? What might happen if you did so?

_____

_____

What might be holding you back from wanting to reboot? What might you lose or miss if you hold back too long?

_____

_____

In what ways do you need to grow in respect for yourself and others?

_____

_____

In what ways do you need to grow in your communication skills?

_____

_____

_____

In what ways do you need to grow in self-control to be able to accomplish these things?

_____

_____

What resources and tools will you use to help you grow in the areas you have identified?

_____

_____

What kinds of things, like ground rules or ways of handling anticipated challenges constructively, do you and your partner need to discuss and agree on before you reboot the relationship?

_____

_____

Chapter 12

Tying It All Together

Seize the moment, and fly!

Sharing My Journey through a "Pathless Land"

As I have indicated elsewhere, I have great respect for the late spiritual teacher Jiddu Krishnamurti, who said, *"The truth is a pathless land."*[xli] So it is ironic that I am sharing suggestions for finding truth, when each individual must take hold of it first-hand, each in his or her own way. The best I can do, and what I have tried to do in this book, is to share my own journey (so far!) in the "pathless land" and to be candid about my own struggles and about the insights they have brought me in my own quest. I have also tried to offer some questions that may help you on your own unique journey to reach your own insights, observations, reflections, conclusions, and enlightened convictions. But the questions may not be the right questions for you right now, or ever, so please stay open to asking your own questions, as well as seeking the answers to those questions.

This book is not, and could never be, an adequate substitute for trustworthy counsel – therapeutic or spiritual – that resonates with your own personal belief system. But this book does sound the call, as Krishnamurti did, for all of us to examine our belief systems for inconsistencies or distortions that hold us back from our full potential for growth in understanding, love, grace, and truth.

Beginnings, Endings, and Change

Among Buddha's reported last words are these: *"Behold, O monks, this is my last advice to you. All component things in the world are changeable. They are not lasting."*[xlii]

Change is hard for many people, and it is not much easier in relationships. We are not conditioned to expect change as an essential part of reality, especially not in the way we think of romance and relationships. The fairy tales always ends with the handsome prince and the beautiful princess getting married and living "happily ever after." The message that we perceive from fairy tales is that a committed relationship is a ticket to happiness, and that once we are aboard the love train, it is all joy and pleasure and no pain, sorrow or unpleasantness. And that is simply not true.

The good news, though, is that we can look at the pains that happen in and through relationships, and think of them as birth pains, signaling the arrival of something fresh and wonderful – a transformed person. Relationship trauma is yin to the yang of forgiveness, and forgiveness brings growth, closure, transformation, and healing. It is a process, not an event, and is likely to happen many times as pain brings reflection, reflection brings insight, and insight brings change.

Hopefully, as we progress, the times of peace and joy in our relationships increase, and our times of sorrow and brokenness decrease. But they are both part of the whole fabric of life-in-relationship, which we cannot escape and which we are foolish to deny.

Even the you+me of "us" involves two ever-changing components. Even if only one person in a relationship undergoes change, the dynamic of the relationship changes. So when you have two people who are changing over time, in different ways and at different rates, it is inevitable that there will be disruption to the status quo of a relationship. To take change as a given, and to expect it, makes it a little easier to handle when it arrives. At the very least, expecting change reduces the element of surprise.

Because we are all works in progress, we are all undergoing this lifelong series of transformations and refinements. We can show respect to one another by responding with patience and grace to other people's seasons of change, and should give ourselves some patience and grace when we are in the transformational cocoon and just emerging from it.

Ruth Bell Graham, late wife of preacher Billy Graham, saw a road sign one time when she was driving through a construction area, and she insisted that the words be inscribed on her gravestone. The words are, *"End of construction. Thank you for your patience."*[xliii] From the moment of conception until we take our final breath, we are construction zones. And construction zones can be very messy and inconvenient places. Hazards exist for those who are not mindful of what is going on all around them. Understanding that people are under construction much of the time, and thinking of interactions as encounters in construction zones, can provide a helpful context for processing what we experience around us in our interactions with other people – from our closest relationships to passing encounters with others. What do I mean? I am less likely to let the grumpy server who handed me my coffee change my mood for the day if I remember that the server is a fellow pilgrim in the construction zone, a work under construction, who may be having a hard day or going through a tough season. I may be more willing to show grace and forbearance to a co-worker, friend or partner who lashes out at me (perhaps precisely because I am seen as trustworthy and "safe"), during a season of pain or hardship. We all have those times. We all need that kind of grace.

Making Change Happen

Who can you change? Ultimately, only you can change you.

The inevitability of change is not an invitation to make your partner change. Well-timed dialogue using open, gracious, respectful communication may help your partner see reflections that he or she wants to change or is willing to change, but it does not guarantee that your partner will change according to your preferences or on your timetable. Furthermore, forcing transformation upon others usually produces feelings of resentment in the one being forced, and any changes in behavior that come about from force or manipulation quickly fall away. Until a person changes from the inside out, behavioral changes are like a mask or a set of clothes – easy to shed when they become uncomfortable.

Transformation that is freely sought and eagerly pursued can bring growth, peace, and amazing relationships that are mutually fulfilling. Such transformation is not easy, but it is change that goes all the way down to the core, to the essence of a person. The changed behaviors and ways of being flow from the transformation that has taken place within.

But transformation is costly and time-consuming. You are, most definitely, worth the time and cost. Your relationship may also be worth the time and cost, but you cannot, single-handedly, change your partner. You cannot drag your partner, kicking and screaming, into a better day. It doesn't work!

If you "Know You'll Never Love This Way Again," then make the costly investment to repair the relationship, as far as it is in your power to accomplish it. Don't hold back, unless the sacrificial investment causes or perpetuates unacceptable damage to you or to others. (In other words, if your life or someone else's life is at risk, because of an abusive relationship, **do what it takes to be safe**. It's hard to have a fulfilling relationship if you are dead or in a coma.)

I caution against breaking up and moving on, lightly or callously, from a relationship in which your safety is not at stake. But if you cannot revive the dead relationship, or if you are not willing to expend the necessary resources to restore it, make every effort to end the relationship kindly, graciously, reflectively, and with forgiveness, striving to land well, so that you can go forward with greater wisdom, wholeness and without regrets. Persistent regrets make old wounds immortal. Don't empower your injuries! Heal from them and grow stronger because of them. And try to help your soon-to-be former partner do the same.

We Can Overcome!

Gymnastics, in general, and the inspiring example of 2012 Olympic gold-medal-winning gymnast Gabby Douglas, in particular, inspired me to think about relationships in terms of take-off, flight, and landing or dismount. While blessed with loving, supportive family members, Gabby Douglas still had to endure the rigors of training to transform her into a focused and disciplined athlete, with the strength of mind, body, and spirit to win Olympic gold. She had to overcome the impact of circumstances like financial hardship, her parents' divorce and physical separation from her family while she was training.

Such hardships can be a refiner's fire that brings forth gold, or it can consume and bring forth ashes. How we respond to the fire and what we do in the fire makes all the difference in the outcome. How do we fly? How do we dismount? Do we stick the landing? Do we end well, so that we are prepared to begin again, even better than before?

Even if you have let circumstances and hardships burn you to ashes in the past, there is still hope for the future. While you still have the breath of life in you, you can still rise up like the phoenix, which was a mythical bird that died by fire and then rose reborn from its own ashes. Every day is a new day that brings a new opportunity to learn from the highly reflective classroom of relationships all around you. Every day is a new chance to process and shed regret in the cocoon, to grow and to heal. Every moment is a new invitation to show respect to yourself and others, to communicate clearly and compassionately, to take responsibility, and to experience and share the freedom of forgiveness.

Seize the moment, and fly!

EXERCISE 14: PUTTING THESE IDEAS INTO PRACTICE

As you reflect on the summary of ideas and opportunities presented in this chapter, please reflect on the following questions.

Who do you trust as a counselor/confidant/ trusted sounding board to walk alongside you, to help you figure out what questions you need to ask yourself and to encourage you to keep processing through the hard stuff, without just telling you what you want to hear or think you ought to hear?

_____

_____

_____

If you chose to consider the questions presented at the end of each chapter and to write responses to the questions, what have you learned from each exercise?

_____

_____

_____

Consider reviewing your responses to the questions you answered after 3 months, 6 months, or a year and make notes (maybe in the margins, with a different colored pen, or in a comment, if you responded in an electronic journal) of anything you see differently or anything that the passage of time has borne out as particularly relevant or true. Note any key insights here.

_____

_____

_____

_____

Describe below how you can celebrate the person you are becoming, and rejoice in how far you have come on the journey.

_____

_____

_____

_____

ZO WILLIAMS'

T.L.O.S.

THE LINE OF SUCCESSION

CUSTOM CLOTHIER

www.iamzowilliams.com

COMING SUMMER 2015

The #ZoWhat? Morning Show!!! Exclusively on TRADIOV.com
Every MONDAY at 11:00 a.m.-1:00 p.m. PST/PDT
Telephone: 855.878.4652

Zo (The Voice of Reason) can also be heard on **Hot Button Radio**
every Monday, WEDNESDAY and FRIDAY from
5:00-7:00 p.m. PST/PDT

Dash Radio is a downloadable APP AVAILABLE FOR
YOUR CELL PHONE at DashRadio.com

ENDNOTES

Chapter 2

[i] Jiddu Krishamurti, "The Mirror of Relationship: Love, Sex and Chastity" (transcript of fifth talk presented at Rajghat, India, 20 February 1949, available from http://www.jkrishnamurti.org/krishnamurti-teachings/view-text.php?tid=305&chid=4635; Internet; accessed 9 March 2015

[ii] John Donne, Meditation XVII, Devotions upon Emergent Occasions Retrieved 3/9/2015 available from http://www.luminarium.org/sevenlit/donne/meditation17.php; Internet; accessed 9 March 2015

[iii] Michael Onyebuchi Eze, "What is African Communitarianism? Against Consensus as a Regulative Ideal," *South African Journal of Philosophy* 27, no. 4 (November 2008): 387 [journal online]; available from EBSCO MegaFILE, EBSCOhost; Internet; accessed 17 January 2014

[iv] William Herschel, "Catalogue of 500 New Nebulae, Nebulous Stars, Planetary Nebulae, and Clusters of Stars; With Remarks on the Construction of the Heavens," *Philosophical Transactions of the Royal Society of London* 92: 481, quoted in "Binary Star," available from http://en.wikipedia.org/wiki/Binary_star; Internet; accessed 9 March 2015

[v] Siedah Garrett and Glen Ballard, "Man in the Mirror" *Bad*, Epic Records, 1987, song information available from http://en.wikipedia.org/wiki/Man_in_the_Mirror; Internet; accessed 7 March 2015

[vi] Negril-Tour-Guide.Com, "Bob Marley Quotes," available from http://www.negril-tour-guide.com/bob-marley-quotes.html; Internet; accessed 10 March 2015

Chapter 3

[vii] Eric Carle, *The Very Hungry Caterpillar* (New York: Philomel Books, 1969)

[viii] Frank Loesser, "Inchworm," *Hans Christian Andersen*, song lyrics available from http://www.johnnymercerfoundation.org/pdfs/FrankLoesserLyricNotes.pdf;Internet; accessed 7 April 2014

^{ix} Charles Hummel, *Tyranny of the Urgent*, (Downers Grove, IL: InterVarsity Christian Fellowship of the United States of America, 1967)

^x Stephen R. Covey, A. Roger Merrill, and Rebecca R. Merrill. *First Things First: To Live, to Love, to Learn, to Leave a Legacy* (New York: Simon & Schuster, 1994) 88-89

Chapter 4

^{xi} Elisabeth Kübler-Ross, *On Death and Dying* (New York: Scribner, 1969)

^{xii} Jennifer Kromberg, "The 5 Stages of Grieving the End of a Relationship," *Psychology Today*, 11 September 2013 [online journal]; Published September 11, 2013; available from http://www.psychologytoday.com/blog/inside-out/201309/the-5-stages-grieving-the-end-relationship; Internet; accessed 9 March 2015

^{xiii} Ervin Drake, Dan Fisher, and Irene Higginbotham, "Good Morning, Heartache," song lyrics available from http://www.azlyrics.com/lyrics/billieholiday/goodmorningheartache.html; Internet; accessed 8 April 2014

^{xiv} Alcoholics Anonymous, "AA Serenity Prayer," available from http://www.aa.org/assets/en_US/smf-129_en.pdf; Internet; accessed 9 March 2015, quoted in 50 Cent, "Gotta Make It to Heaven," Aftermath Entertainment/Shady Records/Interscope Records, 2003

^{xv} 1 Corinthians 13:4-8 WEB (World English Bible); available from worldenglishbible.org; Internet; accessed 9 March 2015

^{xvi} Garrett and Ballard, "Man in the Mirror"

^{xvii} Robert Anton Wilson, "Don't Believe in Anybody Else's BS [Robert Anton Wilson]," YouTube video file posted February 3, 2013; available from https://www.youtube.com/watch?v=zTLkiJUX05A; Internet; accessed 9 April 2015

Chapter 6

^{xviii} Ken Sande, *The Peacemaker: A Biblical Guide to Resolving Personal Conflict*. 3rd ed. (Grand Rapids, Michigan: Baker Books, 2004) 206-09

^{xix} Corlette Sande and Russ Flint, *The Young Peacemaker Student Activity Book*, Vol. 8 (Wapwallopen, Pa.: Shepherd Press, 1997) 8-5

Chapter 8

[xx] Luke 7:47 WEB (World English Bible); available from worldenglishbible.org; Internet; accessed 9 March 2015.

[xxi] "Interview to the Press" in Karachi about the execution of Bhagat Singh (23 March 1931); published in Young India (2 April 1931), reprinted in Collected Works of Mahatma Gandhi Online Vol. 51

[xxii] Steve Goodier, *Prescription for Peace: Sixty-second Readings to Help You Build a Better Life* (Divide, CO: Life Support System Pub., 2000) 29; available from http://www.bennettstellar.org/stellar/admissions/forgiveness; Internet; accessed 13 January 2015

[xxiii] John Greenleaf Whittier, "Maud Muller," *Selected American and British Poems*, Lit2Go Ed.; available from http://etc.usf.edu/lit2go/109/selected-american-and-british-poems/5398/maud-muller/;Internet; accessed 13 September 2014

[xxiv] Romans 12:18 WEB (World English Bible); available from worldenglishbible.org; Internet; accessed 9 March 2015

Chapter 9

[xxv] Wally Palmar, Mike Skill, and Jimmy Marinos, "What I Like About You," *The Romantics*, Nemperor/Epic 1979, song information available from http://en.wikipedia.org/wiki/What_I_Like_About_You_(song); Internet; accessed 16 April 2015

[xxvi] J. Krishnamurti Online, "The Core of the Teachings," available from http://www.jkrishnamurti.org/about-krishnamurti/the-core-of-the-teachings.php; Internet; accessed 12 January 2015

[xxvii] Renard E. Williams, *The Rebirth of Seeds* (Los Angeles: Event-Horizon Publishers, 2005)

Chapter 10

[xxviii] Sade Adu and Stuart Matthewman, "Hang On to Your Love," *Diamond Life*, Epic Records, 1984, accessed April 16, 2015 http://en.wikipedia.org/wiki/Hang_On_to_Your_Love

[xxix] Norman Whitfield and Edward Holland, Jr., "Ain't Too Proud to Beg" Gordy Records, 1966, G 7054, song information available from http://en.wikipedia.org/wiki/Ain%27t_Too_Proud_to_Beg; Internet; accessed 16 April 2015

[xxx] Clifton Davis, "Never Can Say Goodbye," *Maybe Tomorrow*, Motown Records, 1971 MS 735, song information available from http://en.wikipedia.org/wiki/Maybe_Tomorrow_(The_Jackson_5_album); Internet; accessed 16 April 2015

[xxxi] George Cukor, *Gaslight*, Culver City, California: Metro-Goldwyn-Mayer 1944; video recording information available from http://www.imdb.com/title/tt0036855/?ref_=fn_al_tt_1; Internet; accessed 16 April 2015. See also "Gas Light," available from http://en.wikipedia.org/wiki/Gas_Light; Internet; accessed 16 April 2015

[xxxii] See Abraham H. Maslow, *The Psychology of Science: A Reconnaissance* [book online] (Chapel Hill, NC: Maurice Bassett Publishing, 2002); available from www.AbrahamMaslow.com.

[xxxiii] For more about these concepts, see Hinduwebsite.com, "Who Am I? Aham Brahmasmi," available from http://www.hinduwebsite.com/hinduism/essays/mahavakyas2.asp; Internet; accessed 17 April 2015

[xxxiv] Frankie Beverly, "We Are One," *We Are One* Capitol Records, 1983, song information available from http://en.wikipedia.org/wiki/We_Are_One_(Maze_album); Internet; accessed 7 March 2015

[xxxv] Richard Kerr and Will Jennings, "I'll Never Love This Way Again," *Dionne*, Arista Records, 1979; song information available from http://en.wikipedia.org/wiki/I'll_Never_Love_This_Way_Again; Internet accessed 16 April 2015

Chapter 11

[xxxvi] For more discussion on this topic, see How-to Geek.com, "HTG Explains: Why Does Rebooting a Computer Fix So Many Problems?" available from http://www.howtogeek.com/173760/htg-explains-why-does-rebooting-a-computer-fix-so-many-problems/; Internet; accessed 17 April 2015

xxxvii The Parkers, "Funny Funny Valentine," Season 1, Episode 15, first aired on UPN network February 14, 2000. See also episode summary available from http://www.episodedata.com/series.php?id=885: Internet; accessed 17 April 2015

xxxviii For more about the impact of neurochemicals on our brains, see Joe S. McIlhaney and Freda McKissic Bush, *Hooked: New Science on How Casual Sex Is Affecting Our Children* (Chicago: Northfield Pub., 2008)

xxxix Otis Redding, "Respect," recorded by Aretha Franklin, Atlantic Records 2403; song information available from http://en.wikipedia.org/wiki/Respect_(song): Internet; accessed 16 April 2015

xl See Travis Bradberry and Jean Greaves, *Emotional Intelligence 2.0* (San Diego: TalentSmart, 2009) 6-7, 16-17.

Chapter 12

xli J. Krishnamurti Online, "The Core of the Teachings."

xlii See Buddha.net, "The Buddha's Last Words," *Life of the Buddha*; available from http://www.buddhanet.net/e-learning/buddhism/lifebuddha/2_31lbud.htm; Internet; Accessed 17 April 2015

xliii Billy Graham, *Nearing Home: Life, Faith, and Finishing Well* (Nashville: Thomas Nelson, 2011) 95